Lincoln Christian College

P9-DIE-391

GIFT OF GIFTS

by

Edward W. O'Rourke
Bishop of Peoria

PAULIST PRESS
New York/Ramsey/Toronto

Copyright © 1977 by
The Missionary Society
of St. Paul the Apostle
in the State of New York

All rights reserved. No part of this book may be reproduced or trans-
mitted in any form or by any means, electronic or mechanical, including photocopying, recording or by any information storage and re-
trieval system without permission in writing from the Publisher.

Illustrations: George Wuellner

Library of Congress
Catalog Card Number: 77-74580

ISBN: 0-8091-2025-9

Published by Paulist Press
Editorial Office: 1865 Broadway, New York, N.Y. 10023
Business Office: 545 Island Road, Ramsey, N.J. 07446

Printed and bound in the
United States of America

Acknowledgments

Scripture texts used in this work are taken from the NEW
AMERICAN BIBLE, copyright © 1970 by the Confraternity of
Christian Doctrine, Washington, D.C., and are used by license of
said copyright owner. No part of the NEW AMERICAN BIBLE
may be reproduced in any form without permission in writing from
the Confraternity of Christian Doctrine, Washington, D.C. All rights
reserved.

Quotations from *The Documents of Vatican II.* Reprinted with
permission of America Press. All Rights Reserved. © 1966 by America
Press, 106 W 56 Street, New York NY 10019.

231.1
Or7

Contents

Paulist

1.95

19 Aug. '77

56391

*To all teachers of Catholic doctrine
in Catholic schools, colleges,
seminaries and catechetical programs
with gratitude for their services
and with a prayer
for the guidance of the Holy Spirit
in their vocation*

Introduction

A renewed interest in the Holy Spirit is emerging in the Church today. Doubtlessly, the Holy Spirit himself is stirring up this interest. It may be due also to frequent references to the Holy Spirit in the documents of Vatican Council II and to the emergence of a charismatic movement among Catholics, particularly in the United States.

Pastoral Approach

The Holy Spirit, indwelling in and sanctifying the Christian and the Church, is the subject of this little book. My approach is pastoral—an effort as bishop to instruct and motivate the people of the Peoria Diocese and other interested Christians. Since this is a pastoral, I shall omit extensive examination of issues debated by theologians and stress the application of doctrine to the spiritual formation of God's people. I have confined to footnotes quotations from theologians, lest the presentation become too lengthy and pedantic for the majority of my readers. In the text, I offer my analysis of the topic, together with the scriptural passages and quotations from the documents of Vatican II which constitute the chief basis for these views.

The purpose of this book, then, is to nurture response to authentic special charisms but, much more importantly, to urge all Christians, particularly Catholics, to attend and respond to the Holy Spirit dwelling within them. I pray that this little book will occasion a "stirring of the Spirit" within them.

The Trinity and Redemption

The best context in which to consider the actions of the Holy Spirit is the plan of redemption in its relationship to the three persons of the Blessed Trinity. God the Father is the Creator, the source of all things. He is also the goal of creation. Not only do we and other creatures take our origin from the Father, we also are destined to return to him. Only in this reunion with the Father can we find fulfillment and enduring happiness.

But sin disordered this plan. Essentially, sin is a turning away from the Father, a pursuit of some creature in place of him.

Jesus Christ became our incarnate brother in order to remedy sin in the most radical way possible. He is truly the "way," the only way back to the Father. Precisely to the degree that we are one with Christ Jesus, do we participate in his redemptive acts. We sinful creatures find our way back to the Father only through union with the Son.

The Holy Spirit serves an essential role in this plan. He, from the moment of baptism until the day of the parousia, labors to make us more completely one with the Son, and, therefore, capable of finding our way back to the Father.

Chief Truths

The chief truths from which this treatise springs are the following:

1. The Holy Spirit inhabited and sanctified the sacred humanity of Jesus from the moment of his conception. The Holy Spirit contributed powerfully to the resurrection of Christ and filled the glorified Christ with power. Christ's outreach to members of his Church since Easter and Pentecost is only in and through the Holy Spirit.

2. Similarly, the Holy Spirit dwells in and sanctifies Christians and the Church as a whole. His goal is to make the Christian progressively more like Christ, and to make the Church one and holy.

3. Jesus is Lord of all creation precisely because he is filled with the power of the Holy Spirit. Embracing the lordship of Jesus is at the heart of the ideals, morality and mission of all Christians.

4. The Christian, striving to respond to the Spirit, experiences obstacles from the "flesh," the sinful and worldly tendencies within him.

5. The indwelling Holy Spirit, given through the sacraments of initiation during childhood, must be "stirred up" during the years of adulthood. Dispositions such as humility, love, prayerfulness, patience during suffering and support from other believers help bring about this stirring of the Spirit.

6. The greatest service charismatics can offer the Church today is to help make all Christians aware of the indwelling Spirit, the gift of gifts, who dwarfs all other gifts.

7. Bishops and pastors must assist the laity in discerning spirits, in determining which promptings are from the Holy Spirit and which spring from human nature, the environment, etc.

I pray that this little book will be a source of sound instruction for each reader and that the Holy Spirit will powerfully move all to a life of holiness and joy.

I
God in Us

The Holy Spirit is the chief gift given through Christian initiation. All other gifts, spiritual and material, pale into insignificance in comparison to this divine gift. Let us examine the impact of the indwelling Holy Spirit on the individual Christian.

The sacraments of initiation—baptism, confirmation and the Eucharist—effect a marvelous transformation of the Christian. He is changed from a state of sin to a "new creation." He receives a created but very real share in the divine nature and begins in a feeble way to live the God-life.

The Indwelling Spirit

At the same time the Holy Spirit comes to dwell in such a baptized Christian. In the words of St. Peter, "You must reform and be baptized, each one of you, in the name of Jesus Christ, that your sins may be forgiven; then you will receive the gift of the Holy Spirit." (Acts 2, 38) At the Last Supper Jesus promised: "If you love me and obey the command I give you, I will ask the Father and he will give you another Paraclete— to be with you always: the Spirit of truth, whom the world cannot accept, since it neither sees him nor rec-

7

ognizes him; but you can recognize him because he remains with you and will be within you." (John 14, 15-17) Throughout the Acts of the Apostles there are repeated accounts of those who were received into the Church being "filled with the Holy Spirit" or being "overwhelmed by the Holy Spirit" and who as a result lived revitalized, joyful and apostolic lives.[1]

The Seven Gifts of the Holy Spirit

The Holy Spirit indwelling in us carries on activities of enlightenment and strengthening which have been described in the Scriptures and in Christian tradition as the "seven gifts" of the Holy Spirit. Four of these gifts enlighten the mind: knowledge, understanding, wisdom and counsel; three of them strengthen the will: fear of the Lord, piety and fortitude. These gifts are dispositions of the soul corresponding with actual graces which the Holy Spirit gives the Christian in pursuit of these seven aspects of the spiritual life.

I am convinced that, since the gifts of the Holy Spirit are described in Isaiah 11, 2, and have been a part of the teaching of the Church for many centuries, we must not omit them from any authentic treatise of the Holy Spirit.

St. Thomas Aquinas and most modern theologians agree that these gifts of the Holy Spirit are not limited to seven; they are many. In the Scripture the number seven connotes a fullness, a plentitude.

This brief description of the seven gifts reflects the treatise on the gifts found in the *Summa Theologica*, II-II, qq. 8, 9, 19, 45, 52, 139 (I-II, Q. 68). *Knowledge* enables us to see God and his purposes in created things and prompts us to use them accordingly. *Understanding* helps us penetrate more deeply the message of revelation; it does not depend directly on natural learning. *Wisdom* enables us to set goals in keeping with those of God and to order means appropriate to those goals. *Counsel* helps us make correct decisions regarding our own moral actions and to guide others affected by our advice or example. *Piety* literally means love. It prompts us to love and respect God and persons and things related to God. *Fear of the Lord* springs from love of God. It prompts us to stay away from temptation and occasions of sin that might separate us from God. *Fortitude* makes us strong against all the obstacles which may arise in our service of God. The primary goal of these gifts of the Holy Spirit is to make us ever more like Christ our brother. Awareness of these gifts and a conscious effort to respond to them help us to live thoroughly Christian lives.[2]

Hence, we see that the Gospel message is truly "good news." Not only has Christ Jesus become our Emmanuel, our "God with us," but God is in us. He is no longer a distant God—a frightening and impersonal deity. He so loved us that he sent his beloved Son into the world to rescue us from sin and to share his life, his nature and his sonship with us.[3]

The Holy Spirit in Jesus

The New Testament describes in some detail the indwelling of the Holy Spirit in the sacred humanity of Jesus—after which his indwelling in us is patterned. When Jesus was baptized by John in the Jordan "suddenly the sky opened and he saw the Spirit of God descend like a dove and hover over him." (Matthew 3, 16) At the beginning of his public life, Jesus "was led into the desert by the Spirit to be tempted by the devil." (Matthew 4, 1) Early in his public life Jesus "returned in the power of the Spirit to Galilee, and his reputation spread throughout the region. He was teaching in their synagogues, and all were loud in his praise." (Luke 4, 14-15) In the synagogue at Nazareth Jesus identified himself with the "anointed one" described by the prophet Isaiah (61,1-3): "The spirit of the Lord God is upon me, because the Lord has anointed me; he has sent me to bring glad tidings to the lowly, to heal the brokenhearted, to proclaim liberty to the captives and release to the prisoners, to announce a year of favor from the Lord and a day of vindication by our God to comfort all who mourn; to place on those who mourn in Zion a diadem instead of ashes, to give them oil of gladness in place of mourning, a glorious mantle instead of a listless spirit. They will be called oaks of justice, planted by the Lord to show his glory."

Thus, the sacred humanity of Jesus, filled with the Holy Spirit, proceeded to manifest to the world the grandeur of divine love and mercy. He extended special care and attention to the poor and brokenhearted. He went about doing good and healing all who are ill or afflicted.

The indwelling Holy Spirit not only brought power and zeal to the sacred humanity of Jesus; he also brought prayerfulness and joy as we read in St. Luke's account: "At that moment Jesus rejoiced in the Holy Spirit and said: 'I offer you praise, O Father, Lord of heaven and earth, because what you have hidden from the learned and the clever you have revealed to the merest children.' " (Luke 10, 21) The Spirit-filled sacred humanity of Jesus felt a powerful inclination to

commune with the Father in prayer. He frequently re-
treated into desert places to find solitude for this purpose. It was on such an occasion that Jesus taught the
disciples the "Lord's Prayer." (Luke 11, 1-13) Jesus
concluded that exhortation on prayer with the observa-
tion: "If you, with all your sins, know how to give your
children good things, how much more will the heavenly
Father give the Holy Spirit to those who ask him."
(Luke 11, 13)

The prophet Isaiah prefaces his moving description
of the "suffering servant" with the promise: "Upon
[him] I have put my spirit; he shall bring forth justice
to the nations, not crying out, not shouting, not making
his voice heard in the street." (Isaiah 42, 1-4) St. Matthew states that in Jesus this prophecy of the suffering
servant is fulfilled. (Matthew 12, 19-21)

The divinity of Christ Jesus has been so emphasized in our thinking that we may experience confusion
as we read these observations about the indwelling of
the Holy Spirit in the sacred humanity of Jesus. We are
inclined to think of Jesus as all-knowing, all-powerful
and without any need or potentiality precisely because
he is divine. Yet the sacred humanity of Jesus is truly
human, in need of support from the Father, capable of
learning and growth. The Holy Spirit provides for those
needs and affects that growth.

From the moment of his conception, Jesus was
being progressively filled with the Holy Spirit, or, more
accurately, the Holy Spirit which he possessed from the
beginning was being unveiled progressively in him.
This resulted in the sanctification and perfection of his
humanity—shown in a continual loving obedience to his
Father and in loving mercy and service to his fellow
men.

The culmination of this process of sanctification

and perfecting occurred through the death, resurrection and glorification of Jesus. The Holy Spirit's activity in and possession of the sacred humanity of Jesus was tremendously increased as he rose from the dead and was glorified. The resurrected, glorified Christ is a Spirit-filled Christ. "The Lord is the Spirit, and where the Spirit of the Lord is, there is freedom." (2 Corinthians 3, 17) Through his resurrection and glorification, Jesus acquired a new power to bring about the sanctification of his fellow men. "It pleased God to make absolute fullness reside in him and, by means of him, to reconcile everything in his person, both on earth and in the heavens, making peace through the blood of his cross." (Colossians 1, 19)[4]

The Holy Spirit in Us

There is a close parallel between the manner in which the Holy Spirit sanctified and glorified the sacred humanity of Christ and his work of sanctification in us. "If the Spirit of him who raised Jesus from the dead dwells in you, then he who raised Christ from the dead will bring your mortal bodies to life also through his Spirit dwelling in you." (Romans 8, 11)

This process of sanctification by the Holy Spirit and the Spirit-filled Christ results in our sharing in the sonship of Christ as described by St. Paul (Galatians 4, 6-7): "The proof that you are sons is the fact that God has sent forth into our hearts the spirit of his Son which cries out 'Abba!' ('Father!'). You are no longer a slave but a son! And the fact that you are a son makes you an heir, by God's design." This amazing transformation of us is further elaborated in the Epistle to the

Ephesians (3, 16-19): "May he [the Father] strengthen you inwardly through the working of his Spirit. May Christ dwell in your hearts through faith, and may charity be the root and foundation of your life. Thus you will be able to grasp fully, with all the holy ones, the breadth and length and height and depth of Christ's love, and experience this love which surpasses all knowledge, so that you may attain to the fullness of God himself."

This sanctification of us by the Holy Spirit will be culminated on the day of the parousia as suggested by St. Paul in the Epistle to the Philippians (3, 20-21): "As you well know, we have our citizenship in heaven; it is from there that we eagerly await the coming of our Savior, the Lord Jesus Christ. He will give a new form to this lowly body of ours and remake it according to the pattern of his glorified body, by his power to subject everything to himself." "I wish to know Christ and the power flowing from his resurrection. . . . Thus do I hope that I may arrive at the resurrection from the dead." (Philippians 3, 10-11)

Let us not be confused by scriptural passages which refer sometimes to the Holy Spirit and sometimes to the glorified Christ as the cause of our sanctification. The actions of the glorified Christ and the Holy Spirit in our sanctification are inseparable. Since the day of his ascension, Christ Jesus acts in the world only in and through the Holy Spirit. It is a Spirit-filled Christ who gives grace through the sacraments, offers the eucharistic sacrifice, heads the Church, etc. Truly, then, this is the era of the Holy Spirit, the time for interior transformation, a time to "worship in spirit and truth." (John 4, 24)[5]

Keeping in mind this parallel between the indwelling of the Holy Spirit in the sacred humanity of Jesus and his indwelling in us, we shall elaborate in more detail effects of that indwelling on baptized Christians in the chapters which follow.

II
One with Christ

In the past we have been taught to pursue a Christ-centered religion. Now we are urged to pursue a "Spirit-filled religion." Actually, these two proposals are not opposed one to another. Precisely to the degree that we submit ourselves to the promptings of the Holy Spirit will we be truly Christ-centered, will we be more and more like Christ and more effectively witness to him in the world.

Christ-Centered

We are called through baptism to a tremendous transition in our thinking, goals and outlook. We must move from an earth-bound outlook to a spiritual outlook, one centered in Christ. Jesus said to Nicodemus: "If you do not believe when I tell you about earthly things, how are you to believe when I tell you about those of heaven?" (John 3, 12) In the Epistle to the Philippians (3, 17-20) St. Paul points even more dramatically to the contrast between those who "are set upon the things of this world" and those who have their "citizenship in heaven."

It seems that the majority of Christians are only superficially affected by the sacraments of initiation and subsequent religious practices. They are scarcely distinguishable from their non-Christian neighbors in their morals, aspirations and values. Surely, one of the most basic goals of Christian renewal in this post-conciliar period is the correcting and deepening of the Christian's thinking regarding his union with Christ and the implications thereof.

This identification with Christ is progressive. As I have indicated in Chapter I, this is the chief objective of the Holy Spirit dwelling in us. This progression toward union with Christ is often interrupted by sin or indifference. It can be maintained only with a constant life of prayer, of receiving the sacraments and of Christian love.

Lordship of Christ

Acknowledging the Lordship of Jesus Christ is one of the ways we manifest the Spirit. The resurrection and glorification of Christ established his Lordship over all creation. In the words of Jesus: "Soon you will see the Son of Man seated at the right hand of the Power and coming on the clouds of heaven." (Matthew 26, 64) "Full authority has been given to me both in heaven and on earth." (Matthew 28, 18) On the first Pentecost, St. Peter said to the crowd: "Exalted at God's right hand, he first received the promised Holy Spirit from the Father, then poured this Spirit out on us. . . . Therefore let the whole house of Israel know beyond any doubt that God has made both Lord and Messiah this Jesus whom you crucified." (Acts 2, 33-36)

The Lordship of Jesus is a basic theme of St. Paul's Epistles. "Because of this, God highly exalted him and bestowed on him the name above every other name, so that at Jesus' name every knee must bend in the heavens, on the earth, and under the earth, and every tongue proclaim to the glory of God the Father: Jesus Christ is Lord!" (Philippians 2, 9-11) According to St. Paul, the Lordship of Jesus embraces everything and includes a radical reconciliation of all things to the Father: "It is he who is head of the body, the church; he who is the beginning, the first-born of the dead, so that primacy may be his in everything. It pleased God to make absolute fullness reside in him and, by means of him, to reconcile everything in his person, both on earth and in the heavens, making peace through the blood of the cross." (Colossians 1, 18-19)

Regarding our acknowledging the Lordship of Jesus, St. Paul declares: "No one can say: 'Jesus is Lord,' except in the Holy Spirit." (1 Corinthians 12, 3) At first glance, this seems not to be true. Almost anyone can say the words, "Jesus is Lord." Obviously, St. Paul is asserting that no one can say and really mean "Jesus is Lord" without the help of the Holy Spirit. If we really accept the Lordship of Jesus, we must make his goals our goals, his ways our ways. We must keep his commandments and help him reign in all aspects of life and in all parts of the world. This is a sharp departure from conduct on a merely natural plane and, therefore, possible only to those who cooperate with the Holy Spirit and his gifts.

Flesh and Spirit

If we are serious in our determination to observe the Lordship of Jesus, we must recognize and take the right stand in the struggle between the "flesh and the Spirit." St. Paul describes this struggle graphically. "Those who live according to the flesh are intent on the things of the flesh, those who live according to the spirit, on those of the spirit. The tendency of the flesh is toward death but that of the spirit toward life and peace. The flesh in its tendency is at enmity with God; it is not subject to God's law. Indeed, it cannot be; those who are in the flesh cannot please God. But you are not in the flesh; you are in the spirit, since the Spirit of God dwells in you. If anyone does not have the Spirit of Christ, he does not belong to Christ. If Christ is in you, the body is indeed dead because of sin, while the spirit lives because of justice. If the Spirit of him who raised Jesus from the dead dwells in you, then he who raised Christ from the dead will bring your mortal bodies to life also through his Spirit dwelling in you. We are debtors, then, my brothers—but not to the flesh, so that we should live according to the flesh. If you live according to the flesh, you will die; but if by the spirit you put to death the evil deeds of the body, you will live. All who are led by the Spirit of God are sons of God. You did not receive a spirit of slavery leading you back into fear, but a spirit of adoption through which we cry out, 'Abba!' (that is, 'Father'). The Spirit himself gives witness with our spirit that we are children of God. But if we are children, we are heirs as well: heirs of God, heirs with Christ, if only we suffer with him so as to be glorified with him." (Romans 8, 5-17)

   This same theme is rendered even more explicit in St. Paul's Epistle to the Galatians (5,16-26): "My point is that you should live in accord with the spirit and you will not yield to the cravings of the flesh. The flesh lusts against the spirit and the spirit against the flesh; the two are directly opposed. This is why you do not do what your will intends. If you are guided by the spirit, you are not under the law. It is obvious what proceeds from the flesh: lewd conduct, impurity, licentiousness, idolatry, sorcery, hostilities, bickering, jealousy, outbursts of rage, selfish rivalries, dissensions, factions, envy, drunkenness, orgies, and the like. I warn you, as I have warned you before: those who do such things will not inherit the kingdom of God! In contrast, the fruit of the spirit is love, joy, peace, patient endurance, kindness, generosity, faith, mildness, and chastity. Against such there is no law! Those who belong to Christ Jesus have crucified their flesh with its passions and desires. Since we live by the spirit, let us follow the spirit's lead. Let us never be boastful, or challenging, or jealous toward one another."

Flesh in this context refers not only to our bodies but to all our human inclinations of both body and soul in our present sinful condition. We must, according to St. Paul, put to death this old self and let the Holy Spirit and his gifts reign within us. "You must lay aside your former way of life and old self which deteriorates through illusion and desire, and acquire a fresh, spiritual way of thinking. You must put on that new man created in God's image, whose justice and holiness are born of truth." (Ephesians 4, 22-24)

All Christians, charismatics and others, must become more conscious of the Holy Spirit dwelling within them and of their union with Christ Jesus. Even though we begin to live the God-life at baptism, we retain the flesh with all its weaknesses. So long as we remain pilgrims here in this world, there will be a struggle within us. Each of us individually and all of us as a body must strive to lessen the impact of the world upon our thinking and aspirations and to multiply the impact of revelation and grace. A practice of detachment, frequent and joyful prayers and the humble opening of ourselves to the influence of the Holy Spirit are imperative.

III
Witnessing to Christ

Our likeness to Christ, described in Chapter II, should manifest itself in our person and in our actions. Through baptism the Christian becomes a different kind of person. "If anyone is in Christ, he is a new creation. The old order has passed away; now all is new." (2 Corinthians 5, 17) The baptized Christian becomes a new creature precisely to the extent to which he experiences the transformation and incipient glorification that spring from his sharing in the God-life, his union with Christ and his response to the Holy Spirit.

The resurrection and ascension of Christ resulted in his glorification, a situation in which the power, beauty and goodness of his divinity shine forth clearly in his sacred humanity.[6]

Our Glorification

With baptism, a glorication of the Christian takes place on a very limited scale. Throughout his life, the Christian—responding to the Holy Spirit—should become more visibly Christ-like in his person, aspirations, choices, affections, attitude toward suffering, his love for and forbearance toward fellow men, etc. This represents a progressive glorification. This process will culminate on the day of the parousia when, cleansed of sin, our bodies and souls will reflect the glory of the God-life in us in a manner as nearly perfect as possible to human nature.

This personal glorification and witness should lead to public service—a witness in the Kingdom, in the social sphere. The effectiveness of our service to others and their response to our service will be enhanced to the degree that our actions and motives are Christ like.

Christian Love

The root of specifically Christian conduct is a new kind of love. "I give you a new commandment: Love one another. Such as my love has been for you, so must your love be for each other." (John 13, 34) Without the inspirations and gifts of the Holy Spirit, we cannot attain this kind of Christian love. "The love of God has been poured out in our hearts through the Holy Spirit who has been given to us." (Romans 5, 5) Very literally our love for one another must be like the love of Christ for us. This becomes possible as the Holy Spirit helps us remake our goals and conduct according to those of Christ.

This love is vastly superior to mere human love. It is God's way of loving. It can be practiced only by those strengthened by the grace of the Holy Spirit. We can love in this way only because God has first loved us: "Love, then, consists in this: not that we have loved God, but that he has loved us and has sent his Son as an offering for our sins. Beloved, if God has loved us so, we must have the same love for one another." (1 John 4, 10-11)

In the Greek New Testament, this love is rendered with the word "agape." Agape is not sentiment; it involves the will to act. It requires that we love even our enemies. (Luke 5, 27) It must be extended to all men. This love is characterized by spontaneity, tenderness, compassion, completeness and generosity. St. Paul tells us that love embodies many virtues. (1 Corinthians 13, 4) Agape is love among equals; it is never condescending; it uplifts; it helps the beloved to gain freedom and self-respect.[7]

This new Testament morality, therefore, is not imposed by God from without, as was the Old Testament Law, nor yet is it something demanded entirely by human nature from within. It is a progressive adoption of the holiness of God by reason of the transformation of ourselves into Christ through the power of the Holy Spirit: "Those who belong to Christ Jesus have crucified their flesh with its passions and desires. Since we live by the Spirit, let us follow the Spirit's lead." (Galatians 5, 24)

Positive Morality

New Testament morality is essentially positive. Yet, the prohibitions of the decalogue still prevail: "My point is that you should live in accord with the spirit and you will not yield to the cravings of the flesh." (Galatians 5, 16) Now, we must not only avoid sin; we must strive for holiness: "But now Christ has achieved reconciliation for you in his mortal body by dying, so as to present you to God holy, free of reproach and blame." (Colossians 1, 22)

Apostolic zeal is also required of the baptized Christian. He is one with Christ and members of his body. Hence, he must be vitally concerned for the welfare of those members, "that there may be no dissension in the body, but that all the members may be concerned for one another. If one member suffers, all the members suffer with it; if one member is honored, all the members share its joy." (1 Corinthians 12, 25-26)

Not only does the indwelling Holy Spirit help us to live in Christ; he also incorporates us ever more completely into the body which is the Church and of which Christ is the head. Therefore, Christian living is not properly limited to a "God and me" devotion. It is a call to service. The sacraments of initiation require of us a labor in the Kingdom. We, the baptized members of the Church, must remake the whole world and bring all men into the one true fold. We must labor as Christ Jesus did to establish justice, love and peace throughout the world.

This is a difficult and thankless task. The people of the world are not anxious to be reformed. Those who respond to this aspect of the Christian calling find themselves embroiled in a great deal of controversy. Weak individuals tend to abandon this task and hide in a more sheltered kind of religious life.

Perfecting the Social Order

The Fathers of Vatican Council II have spelled out in some detail the areas in which apostolic Christians should labor. Christ, the head of the body, wishes to reign in all areas of life. It is largely the task of the apostolic layman to apply the plan of God and the message of the Gospel to the world of business, agriculture, politics, education, recreation, etc. The following excerpt from paragraph 5 of the *Decree on the Apostolate of the Laity* develops this thought: "The mission of the Church is not only to bring the message and grace of

Christ to men but also to penetrate and perfect the temporal order with the spirit of the Gospel. In fulfilling this mission of the Church, the Christian laity exercise their apostolate both in the Church and in the world, in both the spiritual and the temporal orders. These orders, although distinct, are so connected in the singular plan of God that he himself intends to raise up the whole world again in Christ and to make it a new creation, initially on earth and completely on the last day."

A Living Witness

In the *Constitution on the Church* (paragraph 12) the Council Fathers declare: "The holy people of God shares also in Christ's prophetic office. It spreads abroad a living witness to him, especially by means of a life of faith and charity and by offering to God a sacrifice of praise, the tribute of lips which give honor to his name."

The apostolate, however, is more than a mere collection of services to individuals. It must also include an effort to reform social institutions. The most devastating social ills result not so much from the individual acts of injustice as from systemic disorders such as slavery, racial prejudice, corrupt political systems, disorders in labor-management relations, urban blight, etc. Those who commit themselves to witnessing to Christ must reform these evil systems.

This task almost defies accomplishment. It must involve accurate analyses of the causes of the social disorders. Alternate models must be devised. A significant part of the populace, particularly those who have political, economic and social clout, must be convinced of the desirability of the new model. Efforts to replace the old system with the new must be persevering and accompanied with a constant re-evaluation and read-justment.

Examples of the difficulties in changing evil social systems abound in our times. During the 1960's, many leaders in the private and public sector engaged in a sincere and massive effort to eradicate racism and poverty from the social fabric of this nation. The ingredients of this effort included court decisions and new laws on discrimination and anti-poverty programs on the local, regional, state and national levels. Billions of dollars were expended and millions of persons were involved. Some progress was made toward achieving a more just social system but the goal has not been reached.

Self-Indulgent Reformers

Having been deeply involved in both the interracial justice and the anti-poverty efforts of the 1960's, I can attest to the need for more Christ-likeness on the part of those who attempt to implement these programs. Many of the civil rights and anti-poverty activists who were attempting to correct interracial injustice and to overcome poverty manifest in their own conduct many grievous disorders including hatred, pride, sexual license, vulgarity, etc. There is little wonder that such persons were relatively ineffectual in persuading others to reform their lives.

Mother Teresa

By way of contrast we might attend to the approach of Mother Teresa of Calcutta and her "Missionaries of Charity" to the needs of poor people whom they serve. These sisters are motivated primarily by the fact that they see and serve Christ in the poor. They derive the strength needed for so arduous a task directly from the Eucharist, the Scriptures and community prayers. These sisters are modern exemplifications of the outlook described by St. Paul in his Second Epistle to the Corinthians (6, 4-10): "On the contrary, in all that we do we strive to present ourselves as ministers of God, acting with patient endurance amid trials, difficulties, distresses, beatings, imprisonments, and riots; as men familiar with hard work, sleepless nights, and fastings; conducting ourselves with innocence, knowledge, and patience, in the Holy Spirit, in sincere love; as men with the message of truth and the power of God; wielding the weapons of righteousness with right hand and left, whether honored or dishonored, spoken of well or ill. We are called imposters, yet we are truthful; nobodies who in fact are well known; dead, yet here we are, alive; punished, but not put to death; sorrowful, though we are always rejoicing; poor, yet we enrich many. We seem to have nothing, yet everything is ours!" Truly, God is using the humble and weak persons of this world to confound the wealthy and powerful.

Among the greatest afflictions in the world today are the corrupt governments under which most of the human race lives. It follows, then, that one of the greatest social services is to engage in honest politics and to fill public offices effectively and for the common good. Those who wish to witness to Christ in the public sector might appropriately aspire to political action and public office.

Help from the Holy Spirit

The Council Fathers remind lay apostles of their

dependence on the Holy Spirit in these endeavors: "One engages in the apostolate through the faith, hope, and charity which the Holy Spirit diffuses in the hearts of all members of the Church." Also, some apostolic Christians may be favored with special helps from the Holy Spirit: "For the exercise of this apostolate, the Holy Spirit who sanctifies the people of God through ministry and the sacraments gives the faithful special gifts also (cf. 1 Corinthians 12, 7) 'alloting them to everyone according as He wills' (1 Corinthians 12, 11). . . . From the acceptance of these charisms, including those which are more elementary, there arise for each believer the right and duty to use them in the Church and in the world for the good of men and the building up of the Church, in the freedom of the Holy Spirit who 'breathes where he wills' (John 3, 8)." (*Decree on the Apostolate of the Laity*, paragraph 3)

Not only does the Holy Spirit guide the individual Christian in his own spiritual life and in fulfilling his social obligations; the Holy Spirit also guides the Church as a whole toward its divinely instituted goals. This will be the subject of the following chapter.

IV
The Holy Spirit
Guiding the Church

The Holy Spirit dwells in, inspires and guides, not only the individual baptized Christian but also the Church as a whole. Let us examine in some detail the action of the Holy Spirit in the Church as a whole and direct our attention particularly to the teaching mission of the Church. Let us attend to the relationship between the hicrarchy, the laity and theologians in this task of unfolding deeper meanings of revelation and teaching them to members of the Church and to the world. The division of this task has been discussed extensively in the United States and parts of Europe recently. Perhaps we can detect new developments in this regard.

One of the outstanding features of the New Testament is the indwelling of the Holy Spirit in all of God's people. In the Acts of the Apostles (2, 15-17) St. Peter sees the action of the Holy Spirit on the first Pentecost as the fulfillment of the prophecy of Joel (3, 1) "Then afterwards I will pour out my spirit upon all mankind. Your sons and daughters shall prophesy. Your old men shall dream dreams, your young men shall see visions."

The Holy Spirit in the Whole Church

When the Holy Spirit comes to the Christian in baptism, he progressively assimilates that person into the Church of which the Spirit-filled Christ is the Head. The Holy Spirit dwells in and guides the Church as a whole as well as the individual.

Jesus promised to send the Holy Spirit to the Church as a whole in order to enable it to believe accurately the truths of revelation. "I will ask the Father and he will give you another Paraclete—to be with you always: the Spirit of truth, whom the world cannot accept." (John 14, 17) Jesus does not declare that the Holy Spirit will reveal new doctrines; rather he said: "The Paraclete, the Holy Spirit whom the Father will send in my name, will instruct you in everything, and remind you of all that I told you." (John 14, 26) Later in the same discourse, Jesus assured the apostles: "When he comes, however, being the Spirit of truth, he will guide you to all truth. He will not speak on his own, but will speak only what he hears, and will announce to you the things to come." (John 16, 13)

Inerrancy of the People of God

In his present, glorified, Spirit-filled state, Christ powerfully affects the Church which is his beloved spouse and the instrument with which he spreads the Gospel and builds his Kingdom. Little wonder, then, that those members of the Church who love him and thirst for his truths will be rewarded with a rich grasp of the revealed message and a firm guarantee that their beliefs will be unerring.

The Fathers of Vatican Council II affirm the inerrancy of the Holy people of God in this believing role: "The Holy people of God shares also in Christ's prophetic office. It spreads abroad a living witness to him, especially by means of a life of faith and charity and by offering to God a sacrifice of praise, the tribute of lips which give honor to his name (cf. Hebrews 13, 15). The body of the faithful as a whole, anointed as they are by the Holy One (cf. John 2, 20. 27), cannot err in matters of belief. Thanks to a supernatural sense of the faith which characterizes the people as a whole, it manifests this unerring quality when, 'from the bishops down to the last members of the laity,' it shows universal agreement in matters of faith and morals." (*Constitution on the Church*, paragraph 12)

The Holy Spirit powerfully moves the Church toward unity. At the Last Supper Jesus indicated that unity must be one of the essential marks of his Church and a proof to the world of his mission: " . . . that all may be one as you, Father, are in me and I in you; I pray that they may be [one] in us, that the world may believe that you sent me." (John 17, 21) This unity is brought about first and foremost by love. "God is love, and he who abides in love abides in God, and God in him." (I John 4, 16)

Witness by the Laity

Attending to the special role of the laity, the Council Fathers emphasize the import of witnessing the truths of Christ in the *Constitution on the Church* (paragraph 35): "He [Christ] does this not only through the hierarchy who teach in his name and with his authority, but also through the laity. For this very purpose he made them his witnesses and gave them understanding of the faith and the grace of speech (cf. Acts 2, 17-18; Revelation 19, 10), so that the power of the Gospel might shine forth in their daily social and family life." The Holy Spirit provides the laity with guidance and gifts for the fulfillment of this role: "For the exercise of this apostolate, the Holy Spirit who sanctifies the people of God through the ministry and the sacraments gives to the faithful special gifts as well. . . . From the reception of these charisms of gifts, including those which are less dramatic, there arise for each believer the right and duty to use them in the Church and in the world for the good of mankind and for the upbuilding of the Church." (*Decree on the Apostolate of the Laity*, paragraph 3)

Teaching Authority with Bishops

The Council Fathers make it clear that the ultimate responsibility for authoritative teaching in the Church rests with the hierarchy: "Bishops, teaching in communion with the Roman Pontiff, are to be respected by all as witnesses to divine and Catholic truth. In matters of faith and morals, the bishops speak in the name of Christ and the faithful are to accept their teaching and adhere to it with a religious assent of soul. This religious submission of will and mind must be shown in a special way to the authentic teaching authority of the Roman Pontiff, even when he is not speaking ex cathedra." (*Constitution on the Church*, paragraph 25) In this paragraph the Council Fathers repeatedly assert that the authority of the hierarchy in these matters stems from special guidance by the Holy Spirit. For example: "To the resultant definitions the assent of the Church can never be wanting, on account of the activity of that same Holy Spirit, whereby the whole flock of Christ is preserved and progresses in unity of faith." "Under the guiding light of the Spirit of truth, revelation is thus religiously preserved and faithfully expounded in the Church."

Laity Spread the Faith

Baptism and confirmation call the laity to spread and defend the faith by word and example. "Incorporated into the Church through baptism, the faithful are consecrated by the baptismal character to the exercise of the cult of the Christian religion. Reborn as sons of God, they must confess before men the faith which they have received from God through the Church. Bound more intimately to the Church by the sacrament of confirmation, they are endowed by the Holy Spirit with special strength. Hence they are more strictly obliged to spread and defend the faith both by word and by deed as true witnesses of Christ." (*Constitution on the Church*, paragraph 11)

The Same Spirit in Head and Members

The Council Fathers make it clear also that the Holy Spirit does not contradict himself as he simultaneously guides the hierarchy and the laity: "The Spirit dwells in the Church and in the hearts of the faithful as in a temple. . . . In them he prays and bears witness to the fact that they are adopted sons. The Spirit guides the Church into the fullness of truth and gives it a unity of fellowship and service. . . . In order that we may be increasingly renewed in him, he shares with us his Spirit who, existing as one and the same being in the head and in the members, vivifies, unifies and moves the whole body." (*Constitution on the Church*, paragraph 4)

Consulting the Laity

Let us now examine in the concrete the manner in which the Holy Spirit provides complementary guidance to the hierarchy and laity in their objective of more profoundly understanding revealed truths, teaching them and witnessing to them. Although authoritative statements on matters of doctrine must emanate from the Pope and the college of bishops, these members of the hierarchy come to know more fully the truths revealed by God through listening to and observing the conduct of the laity. Revealed truths become more intelligible, their precious message more clearly discernible, when viewed in the person and activities of the baptized Christians and the living, loving community which is the Church.

Hence, an open communication, based on mutual love and respect, must be maintained between the laity and the hierarchy. Only then can the hierarchy learn the new insights and applications of revelation to the lives of God's holy people today. The Scriptures repeatedly describe the Holy Spirit as a force for unity in the Church.[8] That unity will be endangered if the hierarchy fails to listen to the laity. That unity will be grievously impaired if the laity fail to assent obediently to the authoritative magisterium of the hierarchy.

The role of the laity in the teaching role of the Church today will become more apparent if we attend to the fact that there is a complementary relationship between the action of the Holy Spirit on the laity and that extended to the hierarchy. Whenever preaching or teaching occurs, the disposition of the listener is as important as the knowledge and eloquence of the speaker. The Holy Spirit creates in the disposition of the listener a kind of sifting of truth from error, of the relevant from the irrelevant. We can be sure that those pronouncements of the preacher or of the hierarchy which the Holy Spirit wants as a part of the message will in due time be assimilated and put into practice by the laity.

Common Error Possible

Having so stated, I must emphasize the importance of the phrase "in due time." Both the Scriptures and the history of the Church abound with illustrations of large segments of God's people falling away from truth and manifesting a "hardening of the heart" which prevented their accepting the truth.[9] However, in due time, Almighty God, respecting free choice on the part of the people, brings them back to truth and righteousness.

St. Paul forcefully reminds us of the continuing conflict between "flesh" and "spirit" in these matters. "Flesh" signifies wounded human nature in this pilgrim way. Not every widespread tendency among members of the Church is a reflection of the Holy Spirit's promptings.

Therefore, a complicated task of discernment emerges. The hierarchy of the Church must surely be in touch with the mind of the whole people of God. They must also discern which of the tendencies of a given culture spring from the Spirit and which spring from worldly inclinations. St. Paul admonishes us: "The natural man does not accept what is taught by the Spirit of God." (1 Corinthians 2, 14) These wordly forces today enjoy—through television, magazines, etc.—a very powerful instrument for influencing both individual and collective attitudes.

Balanced Representation

When a bishop attempts to maintain this close communication with members of his diocese, he soon finds that special interest groups clamor aggressively for his attention. Obviously, their demands must be considered in the context of the views of the entire people of God. Structures such as diocesan synods in which there is a broad participation by the whole people, truly representative diocesan pastoral councils, priests' senates, sisters' conferences, etc., help bishops discern the true mentality of the people of his diocese. It follows, of course, that those who participate in these structures should do so prayerfully, with an openness to the Holy Spirit, rather than with a desire to promote their own preferences.

Theologians and the Magisterium

The revealed message is so rich, so magnificent that it must be studied, progressively grasped and applied to daily life. The insight of God's holy people into this revelation expands and grows under the guidance of the hierarchy. However this process is greatly aided by theologians and Scripture scholars. The hierarchy needs the scholarship of theologians in order that an ever deepening insight into revealed doctrine can be gained.

Theologians should never presume to speak for the whole Church. Their conclusions must be adopted by the hierarchy before they can be incorporated into the official body of Church teachings. The hierarchy, on the other hand, must give special attention to the views of theologians precisely because they have professional competence in their respective specialities.

Efforts to understand God's revelation must not be reduced to a collection of human sciences. St. Paul strongly admonishes against "worldly wisdom" in this context.[10] Academic skills are useful in this undertaking, but prayerfulness and openness to the Holy Spirit are vastly more important. I am sure that the vast majority of theologians are doing precisely this.

We may not treat the teaching authority of the Church as if it were merely the collective skills of its scholars. This would do violence to the clear determination by Christ to give teaching authority to the apostles and their successors.[11] It would amount to an ignoring of the most important role of the Holy Spirit as described above. The unacceptability of such assumptions becomes more evident when we recall the extreme limitations in theological skills that characterized the apostles and many of the hierarchy of the early Church.

Through the Church, God has provided an effective and reliable channel of his truths to his people. An indispensable factor in this channel of truth is the Spirit-guided, hierarchical Church in loving and respectful communication with the laity and theologians.

Unity and Love

One of the surest signs of fidelity to the Holy Spirit is unity and love as is suggested by St. Paul in his Epistle to the Ephesians: "I plead with you, then, as a prisoner for the Lord, to live a life worthy of the calling you have received, with perfect humility, meekness, and patience, bearing with one another lovingly. Make every effort to preserve the unity which has the Spirit as its origin and peace as its binding force. There is but one body and one Spirit, just as there is but one hope given all of you by your call. There is one Lord, one faith, one baptism; one God and Father of all, who is over all, and works through all, and is in all." (Ephesians 4, 1-6)

I pray that in the current debate between bishops and theologians concerning their respective roles in the teaching mission of the Church all parties will proceed with "perfect humility, meekness and patience, bearing with one another lovingly."

V
Sacraments of Initiation

Sacraments of Initiation

The Holy Spirit's activities are at the very heart of our relationship with Christ and the Church. Perhaps this relationship will become clearer if we approach them in the context of the sacraments of initiation—baptism, confirmation and the Eucharist.

Membership in the Church is determined primarily by our union with Christ (cf. Chapter II). This union is established by the sacraments of initiation. The Holy Spirit helps bring about this union. He sanctifies the members of the Church to make them more worthy and more effective in God's service.

The Holy Spirit begins his indwelling in the Christian at the moment of baptism. Strictly speaking, his *presence* is not increased through confirmation and the Eucharist; rather his *activity* is increased. Indeed, it is precisely through activity that a spirit effects its presence.

Paschal Mystery

The sacraments of initiation immerse the Christian in the paschal mystery. He shares in and relives the death and resurrection of Christ. He dies with Christ and shares in the God-life, the glory, power and joy of the resurrection. For this reason, the most appropriate setting for these sacraments of initiation is the Easter vigil. In this context we most easily realize that the death and resurrection of Christ is a present reality, experienced again in us who are his body, the Church.

We share in Christ's death and resurrection, not as individuals, but as members of his body, the Church. Each of the sacraments of initiation helps to effect this union with him and his Church. These sacraments, then, are social, for they affect our relations with Christ and one another.

In a special way, the Eucharist is the culmination of our initiation into the Church. Through the Eucharist we are united most intimately with Christ. In the *New Order of Initiation of Christian Adults*, published by the Sacred Congregation for Divine Worship in January 1972, the unity of the sacraments of initiation has been restored, and the order of administering them suggested above, namely, baptism, confirmation and the Eucharist, is observed.

Endangered Unity

Today in the United States (and most of the Western Catholic Church), typically baptism is administered to infants, First Eucharist to children, and confirmation to young adults. This practice of separating the administration of these sacraments into three widely differing times endangers our grasping the unity (around the paschal mystery and identity with the Church) which should characterize this experience.

Many contemporary theologians and liturgists urge that, regardless of the age of the recipients (infants, children or adults), all three sacraments of initiation be administered on one occasion.[12] Admittedly, there are serious pastoral problems embodied in such a practice, just as there are in the practice now in force. This is an issue which requires much study and experimentation.

Service and Maturity

Members of the Church are called, not only to many graces and privileges, but also to serve the Church and the Kingdom. We must, therefore, attend to the social dimensions of this call and strive for maturity in Christ. Apparently some of our separated brethren have overemphasized this commitment to service and striving for maturity in connection with confirmation. In my opinion, we must not let this prompt us to neglect these issues, particularly as we prepare our members for confirmation. Surely at such a time we should be reminded of our social obligations and the manner in which the Holy Spirit helps us to fulfill them.

Even after the sacraments of initiation have been received, the Christian is far from full Christian maturity. St. Paul describes the goal of this process with these words: "Let us profess the truth in love and grow to the full maturity of Christ the head." (Ephesians 4, 15)

Nor is progress toward this goal smooth and always forward-moving. St. Paul refers to the conflict between the flesh and the spirit, between his old, sin-prone self and the new man which the Spirit tries to form in him.[13]

This task of maturation is complicated by the tendency of many Christian parents as well as children to adopt the world's view of maturity which both contradicts and falls short of Christian maturity. This is especially evident in the dichotomy between the quest for power, wealth and pleasure which the world embraces and Christ's example of humility, detachment, suffering and gentleness. The world is not ready to take seriously Jesus' plea: "Learn from me, for I am gentle and humble of heart." (Matthew 11, 29)

Pentecost—Baptism and Confirmation

Holy Mother Church sees baptism and confirmation as accomplishing in us essentially that which was accomplished in the apostles on the first Pentecost. The scriptural passages describing the first Pentecost are rather confusing, perhaps because the events described defy adequate explanation in human terms. The apostles were closer to and more profoundly affected by Christ Jesus after Pentecost than they were when he walked with them in Galilee and Jerusalem. The power of the incarnate Son of God in the world was released in a much greater degree after Easter and Pentecost.

This is due partly to the fact that, after the resurrection, the glorified body of Christ no longer endured the limitations of space and time. Now Jesus can be truly united with persons located in far separated places and in various ages. As we shall note in Chapter IX, it is a part of the divine plan of redemption and sanctification that the activity of the Holy Spirit aiming at uniting us with Christ has been greatly intensified since the day of the first Pentecost.

We, too, after baptism and confirmation, enjoy an

amazing unity with the resurrected Christ and can be the instrument of his powerful love and service to our fellow men. Sadly we must admit that this kind of transformation is not typical of adult members of our Church. In Chapter VII we shall attend in more detail to the steps we can take to "stir up the Spirit" and to respond to the grace which we receive from the laying on of hands.

Appreciation of these exciting insights into the sacraments of initiation is prompting a more effective catechesis in preparation for these sacraments. As a bishop who administers confirmation approximately seventy-five times per year, I can report a gratifying improvement on the part of members of confirmation classes and their parents regarding their oneness with Christ, their relationship with the Holy Spirit and their recognition of their duties as adult Christians. Much more can and must be accomplished in these directions.

The Eucharist

We have previously indicated that our membership in the Church grows as our oneness with Christ increases. Using this norm, it follows that receiving the Eucharist greatly affects our membership in the Church. In the Eucharist we are united with the body and blood, soul and divinity of Christ Jesus. This necessarily brings about a closer union between ourselves and other members of the Church who are similarly united with him. Let us examine more closely the role of the Holy Spirit in the Eucharist and the bearing of the Eucharist on our membership in the Church and our sanctification.

The glorified Christ is a Spirit-filled Christ. This glorified, Spirit-filled Christ sanctifies the members of his Church through sacraments and the eucharistic sacrifice. Or, we may say that the Holy Spirit, acting with the glorified Christ, carries on this work of sanctification. Christ the triumphant "Lord" exercises his sanctifying mission only in the Spirit.[14]

The Eucharist is an activity of the risen, glorified, Spirit-filled Christ, the triumphant Lord. This infers that the Holy Spirit has an integral role with Christ in the sanctifying effects of the eucharistic sacrifice and sacrament.

This is suggested in the prayers immediately after the consecration in Eucharistic Prayer III ". . . by your Holy Spirit, gather all who share this bread and wine into the one body of Christ, a living sacrifice of praise," and Eucharistic Prayer IV: "Grant that we, who are nourished by his body and blood, may be filled with his Holy Spirit and may become one body, one spirit in Christ."

Epiclesis

The Holy Spirit is also intimately involved in the transubstantiation of the bread and wine into the body and blood of Christ as suggested in the "epiclesis" or "invocation" of the Holy Spirit which immediately precedes the consecration in Eucharistic Prayers II, III and IV: "Let your Spirit come upon these gifts to make them holy, so that they may become for us the body and blood of our Lord Jesus Christ" (Eucharistic Prayer II); "We ask you to make them [the gifts of bread and wine] holy by the power of your Spirit, that they may become the body and blood of your Son, our Lord Jesus Christ, at whose command we celebrate this Eucharist" (Eucharistic Prayer III); "Father, may this Holy Spirit sanctify these offerings. Let them become the body and blood of Jesus Christ our Lord as we celebrate the great mystery which he left us as an everlasting covenant" (Eucharistic Prayer IV).

The precise relationship between the Holy Spirit, Christ and the priest-celebrant in effecting the transubstantiation has been a subject of debate between the Byzantine and Western Church for many centuries. I do not attempt to resolve so difficult an issue superficially. However, I suggest that an understanding of the parallel activity of the glorified Christ and the Holy Spirit will greatly reduce the area of disagreement among the debating factions.[15]

Since the ascension, Christ is present in the Church only in and by the Holy Spirit. Hence, the accomplishment of the transubstantiation requires the Holy Spirit's action.

But, since this is a pastoral rather than a theological treatise, let us return to our main concern, namely the sanctification, the "divinizing" of man which is the main purpose of the incarnation and which in a marvelous way is advanced by the Eucharist.

When Jesus ascended into heaven, he did not cease to be present in the world. Rather, he exchanged an historical, exterior presence for a spiritual, interior presence. He no longer stands before men; he lives within them. This happens in a marvelous way when he comes to men in the Eucharist. His goal in this sacrament is to "spiritualize" us, to make us more like him in his glorified state. Without the action of the Holy Spirit this would be impossible.

I am not suggesting that the Holy Spirit somehow replaces Christ in the Eucharist. Rather, since it is the glorified, spiritualized Christ whom we receive in the Eucharist, this great sacrament is the joint activity of Christ and the Holy Spirit.

Thus we see that each of the sacraments of initiation—baptism, confirmation and the Eucharist—unites us to Christ, the head of the Church, and makes us like him. In each sacrament the Holy Spirit and the glorified Christ bring about these great works of sanctification, of "divinization" of the members of the Church.

VI
Charismatic Experiences

"Charism" means "gift." Hence, all Christians are charismatic since they receive the Holy Spirit who is the "gift of gifts," together with his seven gifts and the corresponding actual graces.

Charisms for the Apostolate

The Fathers of Vatican Council II suggest that additional special gifts of the Holy Spirit are widely communicated to the people of God in order that they may fulfill their role in the apostolate: "For the exercise of this apostolate, the Holy Spirit who sanctifies the people of God through the ministry and the sacraments gives to the faithful special gifts as well 'allotting to everyone according as he will.' (1 Corinthians 12, 11) Thus may the individual, 'according to the gift that each has received, administer it to one another' and become 'good stewards of the manifold grace of God,' (1 Peter 4, 10) and 'build up thereby the whole body in charity.' (cf. Ephesians 4, 16) From the reception of these charisms or gifts, including those which are less dramatic, there arises for each believer the right and duty to use them in the Church and in the world for the good of mankind and the upbuilding of the Church. In so doing, the believers need to enjoy the freedom of the Holy Spirit who 'breathes where he wills.' (John 3, 8) At the same time they must act in communion with their brothers in Christ, especially their pastors. The latter must make a judgment about the true nature and proper use of these gifts, not in order to extinguish the Spirit, but to test all things and to hold fast to what is good." (*Decree on the Apostolate of the Laity*, paragraph 3)

Charisms of Office

There are also gifts related to one's office in the Church. With the sacrament of holy orders come gifts such as those of administration, teaching, preaching, discerning of spirits, etc. The fruits of office vary according to the faith, humility, love and prayerfulness of the recipient.

Charismatics

In the Catholic Church today the title "charismatics" is usually understood to refer to those members of our Church (as well as many Protestants) who have experienced the special gifts referred to by St. Paul in his First Epistle to the Corinthians (12, 1-11). "Now, brothers, I do not want to leave you in ignorance about spiritual gifts. You know that when you were pagans you were led astray to mute idols, as impulse drove you. That is why I tell you that nobody who speaks in the Spirit of God ever says, 'Cursed be Jesus.' And no one can say: 'Jesus is Lord,' except in the Holy Spirit.

There are different gifts but the same Spirit; there are different ministries but the same Lord; there are different works but the same God who accomplishes all of them in everyone. To each person the manifestation of the Spirit is given for the common good. To one the Spirit gives wisdom in discourse, to another the power to express knowledge. Through the Spirit one receives faith; by the same Spirit another is given the gift of healing and still another miraculous powers. Prophecy is given to one; to another power to distinguish one spirit from another. One receives the gift of tongues, another that of interpreting the tongues. But it is one and the same Spirit who produces all these gifts, distributing them to each as he wills."

The title "charismatics" is also intended to distinguish the Catholic receivers of special gifts from fundamentalist Protestants who are usually referred to as pentecostals. There are significant differences in doctrine and in practice between the typical pentecostal and the typical Catholic charismatic.[16] Most impressive of these differences is the fact that the vast majority of Catholic charismatics adhere very closely to the magisterium of the Church, want to be very much a part of the whole Catholic community, and seek humbly the counsel of their pastors and bishops. We might also note that the degree of emotionalism characteristic of Protestant pentecostals is usually not found among Catholic charismatics.

Most Catholic charismatics claim a "baptism in the Spirit" which is often occasioned by prayers and the imposition of hands by other members of the charismatic group. Baptism in the Spirit usually includes an abandonment to the guidance of the Holy Spirit which had not previously been experienced by such individuals. It often also includes a special peace of soul and a vital religious zeal. Most who have experienced baptism in the Spirit have a new relish for prayer, particularly community prayer.

A number of Catholic theologians urge that we discontinue using the expressions "baptism in the Spirit" or "baptism with the Spirit" in reference to the experience just described.[17] The reasons are rather obvious. The word baptism literally means to inundate, to thoroughly fill with. In this sense, surely the Holy Spirit baptizes us. Also we note that the expression occurs in the New Testament—for example: "All were filled with the Holy Spirit" (Acts 2, 4); "He it is who will baptize you in the Holy Spirit and fire." (Matthew 3, 11)

In our Church the word baptism means first and foremost the sacrament instituted by Christ in which the pouring of the water is an outward sign for the giving of grace. It would be unfortunate if "baptism in the Spirit" were in anyway confused with this essential sacrament. There is, however, a sense in which the two experiences are related. Most of us receive the sacrament of baptism as infants. Consciousness of the Holy Spirit whom we receive through baptism and abandonment to the will of Christ to whom we are united in baptism must occur at a later date. This might well coincide with an experience such as "baptism in the Spirit." We will have more to say about this important topic in Chapter VIII.

Most Catholic charismatics also speak in tongues. This experience is an exuberant outpouring of praise for God, so enthusiastic that it sometimes lacks the usual discipline of words and sentences. Sometimes it is uttered melodiously, particularly when the speaking in tongues occurs in groups.[18]

Charismatic prophecy is a declaration, seldom about any future event; rather it is usually praise of God, or a declaration of a religious truth, or a statement of counsel, comfort or admonition. Many charismatics claim that their prophecies are prompted by the Holy Spirit. They sometimes speak in the name of God, inferring that God is speaking through them.[19]

Sometimes charismatic prophecies are uttered in languages other than those known to the speaker. Sometimes a second person "interprets" these prophecies and hence exercises another charism, namely that of interpretation.[20]

There is, of course, the possibility of error in these charismatic prophecies. In many instances the charismatic community itself serves as a test for the authenticity of prophecies which are proposed by its members. Ultimately, the hierarchy should have the responsibility to pass judgment on any charismatic prophecies that might affect the Catholic community. This, however, does not happen frequently. The vast majority of charismatic prophecies are in keeping with the teachings of the Church.

The gift of healing can extend to bodily ailments. Most Catholic charismatics limit their healing to religious and moral maladies. They claim in their lives and in the lives of persons they influence significant improvements in faith, fidelity to moral principles, peace of soul, family harmony, etc.

St. Paul indicates: "To each person the manifestation of the Spirit is given for the common good." (1 Corinthians 12, 7) Hence those who receive these charisms should seek ways in which they may be made to serve the needs of other members of the Church.[21]

Charismatics and the Church

All members of the Church can profit from the presence of charismatics among them. Charismatics remind us that prayer should be joyful and engaged in frequently. Their enthusiasm can help correct the excessive coldness of the religion of most Catholics. To those many Catholics who have no awareness of the Holy Spirit's vital role in sanctification, charismatics are a source of useful information and wholesome prodding.[22]

On the other hand, charismatics need close association with other members of the Catholic community. If they become too isolated from the broader Catholic community, there is a danger of their falling into an over-emphasis of certain aspects of their religious experience and the neglecting of other aspects. This is the way in which sects arise. It is for this reason that I have asked the Catholic charismatics in the Diocese of Peoria always to assist at the eucharistic sacrifice in their parishes on Sundays and holydays of obligation. I have also discouraged the separation of charismatics into special enclaves. The other side of this coin, however, is my constant effort to bring other Catholics in touch with our charismatic prayer groups, House of Prayer and other activities.

Cursillo

One of the significant religious movements in the

Diocese of Peoria presently is the cursillo movement which also in our diocese includes TEC (Teenagers Encounter Christ). Most of those who have engaged in cursillo and TEC activities manifest some but not all of the religious attitudes described above. This suggests to me that the division between charismatic Catholics and other members of the Church is very indistinct. It is my earnest hope that, as the years go by, all members of our Catholic community will manifest the best features of charismatics and that charismatics will manifest some of the virtues which have been characteristic of our more traditional Catholics. This, in my estimation, is the way in which the manifestations of the Spirit can best serve the common good.

Currently debated in our Church is the question as to whether Catholics should ordinarily presume that they will experience the special charisms described by St. Paul in 1 Corinthians 12, 1-11 or whether these are to be considered relatively rare experiences.[23] There are rather strong scriptural arguments for the first view; the experience of the vast majority of Catholics down through the ages would argue for the second view. I am not inclined to become involved in this debate. Let us allow the Holy Spirit to move as he will. Of course, with the help of pastors, all of our people will take care to distinguish between genuine and false charisms.

Having acknowledged the many commendable features of the charismatic renewal, a few words of caution are in order. Charismatics stress religious *experiences*. Most of them are laymen and are not deeply founded in *doctrine*; hence, the danger of error. This danger is accentuated when the charismatic group includes fundamentalist Protestants as well as Catholics. A desire for unity sometimes occasions a compromise of doctrine. Similarly some charismatics question the need for the Church, since they have the Scriptures and the Holy Spirit to guide them. These dangers are increased when a charismatic group lacks substantial guidance from the priests and bishop of their area. Pope Paul VI, in his address to the 1975 International Conference on the Charismatic Renewal in Rome, declared that the first principle of discernment of spirits is fidelity to the authentic doctrine of the faith. (See Appendix)

These reflections bring us to the need for discerning of spirits which is the topic of Chapter VIII.

VII
Stir Up the Spirit

At this point one might ask: Why is there so much coldness, sin and apparent lack of sanctity among so many baptized Christians? In response, let us be assured that this is not due to any lack of inspiration by the Holy Spirit. He came into the world at Pentecost, and he came to stay. He continues to do his work of inspiration and sanctification. On the other hand, the Holy Spirit prompts; he never shoves. He whispers; he never shouts. Therefore we can easily fail to respond to the Holy Spirit.

Obstacles to the Spirit

Moreover, it is apparent from the Scripture and from the experience of Christians that an individual can set up obstacles which impede the effectiveness of the Holy Spirit's work in his soul. Among the most tragic of these obstacles are pride and hatred. Those who are filled with pride apparently cannot be trusted with the tremendous powers and with the far-reaching influence on other persons which the graces and gifts of the Holy Spirit bring. Only those who humbly make themselves an instrument of God's will can be so entrusted.

Love

Similarly, since God is love, those who permit themselves to indulge in hatred close their minds and hearts to effective understanding of God, his will and his promptings. Expressed more positively, in order to be more open to the Holy Spirit, we must practice humility in loving exchanges with family and neighbors. In loving community and in loving family life, response to the Holy Spirit is most apparent. Moreover, love for and service of the poor does much to remove obstacles to our response to the Holy Spirit. Let us examine in more detail the manner in which humility and love open one's mind and heart to the inspirations of the Holy Spirit.

Humility

Humility is the virtue which prompts a person to recognize his true relationship with God and fellow men. It is the opposite of pride which frequently shows itself in a presumption of superiority over fellow men and a refusal to accept God's dominion. All racism and most economic and social stratification are rooted in pride and are inimical to spiritual progress.

The Scriptures are replete with passages which affirm the import of humility in making us responsive to the Holy Spirit. "The prayer of the humble and the meek has always pleased thee." (Judith 9, 16) "The Lord is close to the brokenhearted; and those who are crushed in spirit he saves." (Psalm 34, 19) "Every proud man is an abomination to the Lord." (Proverbs 16, 5) "Take my yoke upon your shoulders and learn from me, for I am gentle and humble of heart. Your souls will find rest." (Matthew 11, 29) "He has confused the proud in their inmost thoughts. He has deposed the mighty from their thrones and raised the lowly to high places." (Luke 1, 51-52) "God resists the proud but bestows his favor on the lowly." (James 4, 6)

Pride and a false sense of self-sufficiency shut out grace. The humble person recognizes the limitations of his natural powers and knows that he is completely powerless to produce supernatural acts. Hence, he seeks and cooperates with the inspirations of the Holy Spirit. The Holy Spirit can then use such a person as an instrument through which the power and glory of the risen Christ can be manifested. "This treasure we possess in earthen vessels to make it clear that its surpassing power comes from God and not from us." (2 Corinthians 4, 7)

St. Paul had an experience which bears out this thesis. He had spoken eloquently to the Greeks at the Areopagus in Athens, but had made very few converts. At Corinth he resorted to a simple style of preaching and emphasized the sufferings of Christ. The Corinthians responded enthusiastically. Many of them accepted baptism and became members of the Church. Later St. Paul wrote to them: "As for myself, brothers, when I came to you I did not come proclaiming God's testimony with any particular eloquence or 'wisdom.' No, I determined that while I was with you I would speak of nothing but Jesus Christ and him crucified. When I came among you it was in weakness and fear, and with much trepidation. My message and my preaching had none of the persuasive force of 'wise' argumentation, but the convincing power of the Spirit. As a consequence, your faith rests not on the wisdom of men but on the power of God." (1 Corinthians 2, 1-5)

Late in the eighteenth century a new pastor was sent to a little French village named Ars. This new Curé d'Ars was Fr. John Mary Vianney. Through the priestly labors of this humble man, the village of Ars and a large region of France were revived spiritually. There can be little doubt that the Holy Spirit worked effectively in and through him. Neither can it be doubted that humility was the chief factor occasioning his response to the Holy Spirit. John Mary Vianney had little formal education in his youth. He failed several times to pass his theological examinations in the seminary. He lacked external polish. His humility is well illustrated from one of his prayers: "My God, you have given me all; behold the little that I give you. Give me the strength to give more. My God, here is all—take all; but convert my parish. If you do not convert it, it will be because I have not deserved it."[24]

One of the most humble persons I have ever met is a priest in a midwestern diocese who has provided unprecedented leadership and inspiration in the lay apostolate. He speaks quietly, makes great demands on himself, lives austerely and trusts in God, not himself. Yet I once observed him as he spoke softly to an impressive assembly of university professors and students. His topic was the mystical body of Christ. The audience was electrified by what he said. This, in my estimation, was an illustration of Jesus' remark: "The Holy Spirit will teach you at that moment all that should be said." (Luke 12, 12)

I think also of a young woman, a member of a lay apostolic group in one of the southern states. She has labored behind the scenes for several years in a cooperative whose members are very poor. It can be safely stated that the organization would have failed without her assistance, yet she never claims credit or attracts attention to herself. In trying to analyze the reasons for her great influence on others, I conclude that it is due to several closely related virtues. Her selflessness breaks down the suspicions and jealousies that might otherwise thwart an undertaking of this sort. Her efforts are strengthened by an unusual love and diligence which apparently are founded on her Christian commitment. In my estimation, she is closely cooperating with the inspirations of the Holy Spirit.

Love for the Poor

As we indicated above, love for one's neighbor is one of the dispositions that opens the mind and heart to the inspirations of the Holy Spirit. A classical illustration of this point can be found in the life of St. Francis of Assisi. As a young man he was quite worldly. His conversion to the more devout life was greatly accelerated one day when he was approached by a leper who was seeking alms. Francis gave the man alms but in a rather cold and impersonal manner. As the leper walked away, Francis felt ashamed of his conduct and went to the leper and embraced him. This marked a very significant new response on the part of St. Francis to the inspirations of the Holy Spirit.

Love for the poor and ostracized is especially effective in this regard. Both Old and New Testament inspired writers contend that poverty can dispose a person to accept grace. The poor are usually aware of their material needs and do not find it difficult to humbly seek God's spiritual gifts. "This is the one whom I approve: the lowly and afflicted man who trembles at my word." (Isaiah 66, 2) "Jesus said to his disciples, 'I assure you, only with difficulty will a rich man enter into the kingdom of God.' " (Matthew 19, 23)

But the majority of Christians in our nation are not poor. The experience of many apostolic persons who have engaged in the current war on poverty indicates that openness to the Holy Spirit often results among those who truly love the poor, identify with them, share their sufferings and help them help themselves. Very closely akin to the love for the poor is love for racial minorities and sharing their hopes and sufferings. The fracturing of the human family into separate racial ghettos is diametrically opposed to the dictates of humility and love. Those who labor for interracial justice and thus heal these fractures often become more responsive to the Holy Spirit. The fact that such persons are often subjected to abuse and injury may further explain their responsiveness to the Holy Spirit. Those who participated in the Selma march often refer to the "spirit of Selma." For many it was a spiritual experience which they believe was due partly to the Holy Spirit.

Among the lay apostolic groups with whom I have been associated, the group that is most responsive to the inspiration of the Holy Spirit is the one that practices poverty and identifies with the poor most completely. This group relies largely upon donated food, clothing and money for its support. They give the poor first choice of their food and clothing; members of the group use whatever remains. Their response to the Holy Spirit is such that in every crisis they first seek his guidance and then devise means to implement his promptings. Most Christians first attempt their own solution to problems and then pray for assistance.

It has been my privilege to counsel and cooperate with several hundred young men and women who perform voluntary services among racial minorities and low-income people at home and abroad. I am repeatedly impressed with the spiritual growth of these volunteers while they are engaged in these projects. They become less self-centered, almost incapable of pettiness, more effective as leaders and fortified with a great inner peace.

Typical of this group is a young man who lost his life while doing education and community development work in Vietnam. After his death, a piece of paper was found in his pocket on which the following thoughts were expressed:

By the way of Bethlehem, lead us, O Lord, to newness of life.

By the innocence of the Christ Child, renew our simple trust.

By the tenderness of Mary, deliver us from cruelty and hardness of heart.

By the patience of Joseph, save us from all rash judgments and ill-tempered action.

By the shepherds' watch, open our eyes to the signs of thy coming.

By the wise men's journey, keep our searching spirits from fainting.

By the music of the heavenly choir, put to shame the clamor of the earth.

By the shining star, guide our feet into the way of peace.

During the 1960's, an unusually effective apostolic

team was assembled in a community in the deep south to labor for the welfare of the poor Negroes of the area. Included on this team were fifteen members of a lay apostolic organization, six priests, four nuns, five students from a Catholic women's college and a dozen young women from several high schools and colleges.

They worked and prayed together for three months with marked success. They conducted a fine Head Start program for local pre-schoolers, taught adult classes in English, performed works of mercy among the poor families and laid the foundations for a now-thriving anti-poverty program in the area. The heat was sometimes oppressive and there was some harassment by local segregationists. Yet this was a work of love; it was rewarding, and almost everyone in this group grew spiritually as a result of participating in a special sort of community life and apostolic endeavor.

A growing number of lay apostles have derived motivation from cursillos which are "little courses in Christian living." These four-day spiritual exercises differ from ordinary retreats principally in the extent to which they are an experience in dialogue and loving community. Unlike retreatants who observe silence, those who make cursillos discuss every conference with one another. They try to formulate bonds of love, communication and understanding among themselves. Many persons who have made cursillos are convinced that the Holy Spirit is especially active on these occasions. Indeed, some of the "professores," the laymen who present conferences at cursillos, are possibly charismatic in their dedication to their tasks. They manifest a degree of love, courage and patience out of proportion to the human resources at their disposal. It seems, therefore, not unreasonable to believe that the Holy Spirit is supplementing their natural talents.

Family Life

Similarly, many couples have found in family life the means of making themselves responsive to grace. Christian family life involves unselfish love for spouse and children and many tasks which require humility on their part. When supported by the sacrament of matrimony and frequent prayers, this way of life greatly increases a person's spiritual receptivity. This is an illustration of loving community at its best. A growing number of couples are participating in the Christian Family Movement. Such couples combine their love for family with apostolic motives. This usually provides a fertile soil for spiritual progress.

Religious Life

So also, nuns, priests and brothers who live a community life can dispose themselves for the Holy Spirit's conversion by love for their fellow religious and sacrifices involved in community life. St. Teresa of Avila developed a marvelous receptivity to the Holy Spirit's inspirations in this way as is evident in her writings.

Loving community also nurtures spiritual growth. It is difficult to develop the spiritual life in isolation from fellow men. Christianity is a corporate religion. Love is the first commandment. When love is exchanged, it grows. I have observed many instances in which apostolic Christians bind themselves together in a loving community and thus become more effective in their apostolate and more open to the inspirations of the Holy Spirit.

From the Scriptures and the experience of the Church it is apparent that Jesus calls from time to time to special union with him people who live a community life and practice the evangelical counsels of chasity, poverty and obedience. When an individual responds to these "evangelical counsels," progress in his union with Christ and in his response to the Holy Spirit grows. When the evangelical counsels are embraced as a permanent way of life through the sacred vows of the religious life to chastity, poverty and obedience, the likelihood of profound spiritual growth becomes even greater.

For obvious reasons, excessive attachment to material possessions and sensual pleasures occasion sin, which destroys the life of grace within us and serves as an obstacle to positive progress toward union with Christ. In these days in which materialism and sensuality are so widespread and so vigorously promoted by the mass media, this admonition is worthy of careful consideration.

The stirring up of the Spirit to which we refer in this chapter is primarily a response to the sanctifying grace and indwelling of the Holy Spirit which is brought to us through the sacraments of initiation. For most of us there is a considerable time lapse between our receiving these sacraments and our reaching that degree of maturity which permits the thorough "living in Christ" of which we are speaking. Hence, we must look for means through which we may more effectively stir up the Spirit within us. Traditional spiritual exercises such as missions and retreats and frequent participation in the eucharistic liturgy are certainly among the most effective means for these purposes. Some persons find participation in a cursillo or in a charismatic prayer group similarly useful. Whatever means we employ, we must be aware that our posture is that of the petitioner, of the one who is opening himself to the Spirit, of the one who is trying to respond to a divine impulse. We Americans are so prone to take the initiative, so committed to noisy, bustling activity, that we find it difficult to be truly open, to adopt that degree of quiet, humility and reflection which is necessary to attain to these ideals.

Prayer

This brings us to the final means of stirring up the Spirit within us, namely, prayer. We must earnestly *petition* the Holy Spirit to sanctify us—to make us one with the glorified Christ. The Holy Spirit blows where he wills. (John 3, 8) However, his choice to move an individual or group powerfully is often in response to devout, persevering prayer.

It is useful, as we try to open ourselves to the Spirit, to accept the counsel of a spiritual adviser. Such spiritual advisers must "discern spirits." This brings us, then, to the subject of the following chapter.

VIII
Discerning Spirits

VII
Discerning Spirits

Discernment of spirits is an art by which an individual becomes aware of various spiritual movements within himself and evaluates them as coming from God or coming from some lesser source, either good or evil.

Discernment in the New Testament

The New Testament includes instructions and admonitions concerning discernment of spirits. We read in the First Epistle of St. John: "Beloved, do not trust every spirit, but put the spirits to a test to see if they belong to God, because many false prophets have appeared in the world. This is how you can recognize God's Spirit: every spirit that acknowledges Jesus Christ come in the flesh belongs to God while every spirit that fails to acknowledge him does not belong to God." (1 John 4, 1) The Synoptic Gospels abound with illustrations of holy persons exercising discernment. Mary is able to discern in the words of Gabriel the will of God in her behalf. (Luke 1, 35) So also St. Joseph, from his encounter with an angel in a dream, was able to arrive at a firm conviction that the child conceived in Mary was by the Holy Spirit. (Matthew 1, 18-20) Zechariah shows himself less prompt and certain in his response to divine communications and seeks a sign. (Luke 1, 20) Elizabeth and Simeon are prompted by the Holy Spirit to recognize the promised Messiah in the child Jesus. (Luke 1, 40; 2, 26)

John the Baptist indicates directives for discernment in his preaching. The fact that a person is a descendant of Abraham is not sufficient. Each one must live a fruitful life. John calls for a reform of life as a necessary condition for accepting the Messiah and his message. (Matthew 3, 1-12) As we indicated in Chapter I, the Holy Spirit was a powerful force for the sanctification of the sacred humanity of Jesus, and it was directly in response to the Holy Spirit's prompting that Jesus initiated his public life. Jesus is able very clearly to discern the falsity and evil of the temptations of the devil in the desert. (Matthew 4, 1-11)

In the Sermon on the Mount it is suggested that in order for us to know and understand God's message, we must completely abandon ourselves to him very much as a child does to his father. (Matthew 6, 19-34) Jesus in his evaluation of the mission of John the Baptist asks: "What did you go out to the wasteland to see—a reed swaying in the wind? Tell me, what did you go out to see—someone luxuriously dressed? Remember, those who dress luxuriously are to be found in royal palaces. Why then did you go out—to see a prophet? A prophet indeed, and something more!" (Matthew 11, 7-9) Jesus is suggesting that the life style of John the Baptist is a way to discern the sincerity of his preaching.

In a sense the entire text of the Synoptic Gospels is a demonstration of the divine sonship and messianic mission of Jesus. The pages of the Synoptic Gospels show how discernment of this basic fact slowly unfolds. Apparently Peter is the first to arrive firmly and explicitly at this conclusion. In response to the question by Jesus "Who do people say that the Son of Man is?" Peter replies: "You are the Messiah, the Son of the living God!" Jesus indicates that this discernment was accomplished with divine help: "Blest are you, Simon son of John! No mere man has revealed this to you, but my heavenly Father." (Matthew 16, 13-17)

Jesus indicates repeatedly as the passion approaches that willingness to accept suffering and sharing his cross will be a way to discern the true disciple from the false. "Jesus then said to his disciples: 'If a man wishes to come after me, he must deny his very self, take up his cross, and begin to follow in my footsteps.' " (Matthew 16, 24)

The Early Church

The Acts of the Apostles gives abundant evidence of the powerful way in which the Holy Spirit guided the early Church. The Holy Spirit reaffirms the basic principle mentioned above, namely the necessity of embracing the cross. The early Church experiences persecution but finds in each such experience a new insight to God's will and a deeper joy. "The apostles for their part left the Sanhedrin full of joy that they had been judged worthy of ill-treatment for the sake of the Name." (Acts 5, 41) During these first days of the Church the authenticity of the words and actions of the apostles was confirmed by miracles and special charisms. (Acts 2, 43; 5, 12; 2, 4) Although in the Acts of the Apostles we do not find a clear formula for the discernment of spirits, it is interesting to note that the actions of the Holy Spirit described in Acts result in the fruits of the

Holy Spirit as listed by St. Paul. (Galatians 5, 22-24)
The early Christians described in Acts clearly manifest
love, joy, peace, patient endurance, kindness, generosity, faith, mildness and chastity.

St. Ignatius

Down through the ages, Fathers and saints of the
Church have written extensively about the discernment
of spirits. For our purpose, perhaps the most useful
source will be the reflections of St. Ignatius on this
topic, found particularly in his little book *The Exercises.* [25]

Utilizing these rich scriptural and ecclestical resources, let us attempt to put together a simple and
useful set of directives for the discernment of spirits
today. The basic principle of discernment is Jesus' dic-
tum: "You will know them by their deeds." (Matthew
7, 16) An authentic Christian experience will eventually
prove itself in service to others, in morally sound conduct, in loving family life, etc.

Fruits of the Spirit

The fruits of the Holy Spirit described by St. Paul
(Gal. 5, 22) also provide tests for the authenticity of
religious experiences. If the result of these experiences
is an increase of love, joy, peace, patient endurance,
kindness, generosity, faith, mildness and chastity, we
can reasonably attribute them to the Holy Spirit. If, on
the other hand, the result is anger, disobedience, immo-

rality, pride, etc., we must conclude that the Holy Spirit is not the origin.

In Chapter III I have stressed the importance of witnessing Christ as a manifestation of our response to the Holy Spirit and our union with Christ. The degree to which an individual devotes himself in service to the Church and to individuals, particularly the poor, gives some indication of the authenticity and depth of his religious experience.

A person experiencing a religious renewal rightly attempts first to shore up his union with God in contemplation and spiritual exercises. However, in due time his love for God must overflow into love for neighbor. As indicated above, willingness to embrace Christ's cross is also an essential requirement for anyone claiming to "live in the Spirit."[26]

The several dispositions described in Chapter VII which open the mind and heart to the inspirations of the Holy Spirit also serve as norms for discernment. If the person in question is humble, loving, generous to the poor, prayerful and chaste, he is probably responding faithfully to the promptings of the Holy Spirit.

Three Levels of Discernment

Discerning of spirits can be exercised on three levels: (a) a person may discern spirits within himself; (b) he may counsel another person, helping him to discern spirits within himself; (c) he may discern spirits operative in a group. In each of these three situations the same basic principles should guide us.[27] We should note, however, that regarding counseling other persons, the counselor should never attempt to replace that individual's conscience by his own decisions or urgings. He should rather assist the other party better to understand the principles of discernment and more accurately to evaluate his experiences accordingly.

Discernment of spirits operative in a group becomes more urgently needed as we multiply various group activities in the Church. One of the best ways to assure the group's conformity with God's will is to begin such meetings with devout and extended prayer. If a group begins a meeting with their minds and hearts filled with worldly concerns, ambitions and feelings, that which emerges from such a meeting will probably be worldly in its character.

In order that a priest may safely and effectively provide discernment of spirits to charismatics, it is essential that he inform himself about the basic facts of the charismatic movement. Lacking such facts, he is inclined to one of two errors: he may withhold counsel lest that which he does not understand might be authentic, or he may be guilty of the stifling of the Spirit about which St. Paul warns in 1 Thessalonians 5, 19.

In the *Decree on the Apostolate of the Laity*, paragraph 3, the Council Fathers state: "Believers need to enjoy the freedom of the Holy Spirit who 'breathes where he wills.' (John 3, 8) At the same time, they must act in communion with their brothers in Christ, especially with their pastors. The latter must make a judgment about the true nature and proper use of these gifts, not in order to extinguish the Spirit, but to test all things and hold fast to what is good."

IX
Pentecost Is Now

This is the era of the Holy Spirit, or, in other words, the era of the Spirit-filled Christ. When Christ ascended into heaven, a major phase of the redemption plan was completed. Public teachings, miracles, establishing the Church, instituting the Sacrifice of the Mass and the sacraments, death on Calvary followed by a glorious resurrection—these external, public acts characterized the first phase of the redemption plan.

On the day of Pentecost the Holy Spirit inaugurated the present phase of that plan. He came once, and he came to stay. The era of the Holy Spirit extends from Pentecost until today and on to the end of time. Truly, then, Pentecost is now.

Christ indicated our need for the Holy Spirit and the importance of this phase of the redemption plan: "It is much better for you that I go. If I fail to go, the Paraclete will never come to you, whereas if I go, I will send him to you." (John 16, 7)

The Holy Spirit is accomplishing an interior work, an enlightening of minds and a strengthening of wills. Christ declared: "When he comes, however, being the Spirit of truth, he will guide you to all truth." (John 16, 13)

One of the distinctive characteristics of the New Testament is the fact that special inspirations of the

Holy Spirit are now offered to all the faithful: "It shall come to pass in the last days, says God, that I will pour out a portion of my spirit on all mankind." (Acts 2, 17; cf. Joel 2, 28) In the Old Testament, special inspirations were offered only to prophets, kings and other selected persons.

A New Pentecost

Recent Popes have called for a "new Pentecost." It is my earnest hope that this little book will provide information and inspiration that will hasten the advent of the new Pentecost.[28] This author is convinced that the charismatic movement is one of the several spiritual resources which God in his goodness is nurturing for this holy purpose. Most urgently I suggest that openness to the Holy Spirit and a consequent powerful awareness of unity with Christ Jesus is the calling, not of a favored few charismatics, but of every baptized member of the Church. I pray for the day in which the Holy Spirit's guidance of both the Church and its individual members will be humbly and enthusiastically accepted.

Appendix

Declarations of Pope Paul VI
and the American Bishops

Address of Pope Paul VI to a General
Audience, October 12, 1966. Translation
from *The Pope Speaks* 12, (1967), pp. 79-81

On what does the Church live? The question is
addressed to that which is the internal principle of its
life; the original principle which distinguishes the
Church from every other society; an indispensable principle, just as breathing is for man's physical life; a divine principle which makes a son of earth a son of
heaven and confers on the Church its mystical per-
sonality: the Holy Spirit. The Church lives on in the
Holy Spirit. The Church was truly born, you could say,
on the day of Pentecost. The Church's first need is
always to live Pentecost.

The Council Doctrine

Listen to what the Council says: ". . . the Holy
Spirit was sent on the day of Pentecost. He was to
sanctify the Church unceasingly and thus enable all

believers to have access to the Father through Christ and in one Spirit (cf. Ephesians 2, 18). He is the Spirit of life, a fountain of water springing up into life eternal (cf. John 4, 14; 7, 38-39). . . . The Spirit dwells in the Church and in the hearts of the faithful, as in a temple (cf. 1 Corinthians 3, 16; 6, 19). . . . He introduces the Church to every truth, makes it one in its communion and ministry, provides it with various hierarchical and charismatic gifts, directing it through them, and adorns it with his fruits."

It is in the Holy Spirit that the twofold union is perfected—that of the Church with Christ and with God, and that of the Church with all its members, the faithful. It is the Holy Spirit who gives life to the whole body of the Church and to its individual members by means of that intimate action which we call grace. We are all firmly convinced of this theological truth of our faith, even if it isn't easy for us to form an adequate concept of the ontological and psychological reality to which it corresponds.

But this is enough for us now, and we can say: If the Church lives on the illuminating and sanctifying inspiration of the Holy Spirit, then the Church has a need of the Holy Spirit: a basic need, an existential need, a need that cannot be satisfied with illusions, with substitutes ("sine tuo numine nihil est in homine"—without thy grace there is nothing in man, as the beautiful Pentecost sequence puts it), a universal need, a permanent need.

At this point, someone might raise the objection: But doesn't the Church already possess the Holy Spirit? Isn't this need already satisfied? Yes, of course, the Church already and forever possesses the Holy Spirit.

But first of all, his action admits of various degrees and circumstances, so that our action is needed, too, if the activity of the Holy Spirit is to be free and full; and secondly the Holy Spirit's presence in individual souls can diminish or be missing entirely. This is why the Word of God is preached and the sacraments of grace are distributed; this is why people pray and why each individual tries to merit the great "gift of God," the Holy Spirit, for himself and for the whole Church.

Practical Consequence

For this reason, if we really love the Church, the main thing we must do is to foster in it an outpouring of the divine Paraclete, the Holy Spirit. And if we accept the ecclesiology of the Council, which lays so much stress on the action of the Holy Spirit in the Church—as we likewise note in the traditional ecclesiology of Greek theology—then we should be glad to accept its guideline for fostering the Church's vitality and renewal, and for orientating our own personal Christian lives along these lines.

Where does this guideline lead us? Toward the Holy Spirit, we repeat—which means toward the mystery of the Church, toward the vital communion which the Father in his infinite and transcendent goodness wanted to establish through Christ, in the Spirit, with the human soul and with believing and redeemed mankind, the Church. In other words, it leads us toward the search for and the attainment of God; toward theological truth; toward faith which discloses to us the religious order of salvation.

Some people have preferred to see in the Council an orientation of the Church in what might be called a horizontal direction—toward the human community that makes up the Church; toward the brothers still separated from us who are the object of our longing and are called to the same perfect communion; toward the world around us, to which we must carry the message of our faith and the gift of our charity; toward earthly realities which must be recognized as good and worthy of being taken up in the light of the Kingdom of God.

All this is very true and very beautiful; but we mustn't forget what we might call the vertical orientation, which the Council reaffirmed as primary for interpreting God's design for the destiny of mankind and for explaining the Church's mission in time. God—his mystery, his charity, his worship, his truth, the expectation of him—always remains in first place. Christ, mediator between man and God, is the necessary redeemer who binds together all of our capacity for love and dedication. The Spirit, who makes us Christians and raises us to supernatural life, is the true and profound principle of our interior life and of our external apostolic activity.

The Interior Life

And if we follow this unmistakable orientation, where are we directed? Where are we led? We are guided and led to the interior life; to that interior life—of recollection, silence, meditation, absorption of God's word, spiritual exercise—which seems to annoy some people (we say this with amazement and with sorrow), some beloved sons of the Church. They act as if the interior life were an outgrown phase of pedagogy no longer needed for a Christian life, which the world offers us, as if—relying on this alone and deprived of the protective and strengthening force of interior grace —we could, with our poor forces, succeed in mastering and redeeming it.

No. If we want to be wise and give the Church what it needs most of all, the Spirit, then we must be prompt and faithful in keeping the fixed appointment for a vivifying encounter with him, which is the interior life.

May our apostolic blessing guide and strengthen you for this.

Address of Pope Paul VI to Participants
in the International Charismatic Leaders'
Conference, Rome, October 10, 1973
(*L'Osservatore Romano*, English Edition,
October 11, 1973)

We are very interested in what you are doing. We have heard so much about what is happening among you. And we rejoice. We have many questions to ask you but there is no time.

And now a word to the members of the Grottaferrata congress.

We rejoice with you, dear friends, at the renewal of spiritual life manifested in the Church today, in different forms and in various environments. Certain common notes appear in this renewal: the taste for deep prayer, personal and in groups, a return to contemplation and an emphasizing of praise of God, the desire to devote oneself completely to Christ, a great availability for the calls of the Holy Spirit, more assiduous reading of Scripture, generous brotherly devotion, the will to make a contribution to the service of the Church. In all that, we can recognize the mysterious and discreet work of the Spirit, who is the soul of the Church.

Spiritual life consists above all in the exercise of the virtues of faith, hope and charity. It finds its foundation in the profession of faith. The latter has been entrusted to the pastors of the Church to keep it intact and help it to develop in all the activities of the Christian community. The spiritual lives of the faithful, therefore, come under the active pastoral responsibility of each bishop in his own diocese. It is particularly opportune to recall this in the presence of these ferments of renewal which arouse so many hopes.

Even in the best experiences of renewal, moreover, weeds may be found among the good seed. So a work of discernment is indispensable; it devolves upon those who are in charge of the Church, "to whose special competence it belongs, not indeed to extinguish the Spirit, but to test all things and hold fast to that which is good (cf. 1 Thessalonians 5, 12. 19-21)" (*Lumen Gentium*, 12). In this way the common good of the Church, to which the gifts of the Spirit are ordained (cf. 1 Corinthians 12, 7), makes progress.

We will pray for you that you may be filled with the fullness of the Spirit and live in his joy and in his holiness. We ask for your prayers and we will remember you at Mass.

Address of Pope Paul to the International
Conference on the Renewal Conference in the
Catholic Church, Rome, May 19, 1975
(Official English Translation from French Text)

You have chosen the city of Rome in this Holy
Year to celebrate your Third International Congress,
dear sons and daughters; you have asked us to meet
you today and to address you: you have wished thereby
to show your attachment to the Church founded by
Jesus Christ and to everything that this See of Peter
represents for you. This strong desire to situate yourselves in the Church is an authentic sign of the action of
the Holy Spirit. For God became man in Jesus Christ, of
whom the Church is the mystical body; and it is in the
Church that the Spirit of Christ was communicated on
the day of Pentecost when he came down upon the
apostles gathered in the "upper room," "in continuous
prayer," with Mary, the Mother of Jesus (cf. Acts 1,
13-14).

As we said last October in the presence of some of
you, the Church and the world need more than ever
that "the miracle of Pentecost should continue in history" (*L'Osservatore Romano*, 17 October 1974). In fact,
inebriated by his conquests, modern man has finished
by imagining, according to the expression used by the
last Council, that he is free "to be an end unto himself,
the sole artisan and creator of his own history" (*Gau-
dium et Spes*, 20). Alas! Among how many of those
very people who continue by tradition to profess God's
existence and through duty to render him worship has
God become a stranger in their lives!

Nothing is more necessary to this more and more secularized world than the witness of this "spiritual renewal" that we see the Holy Spirit evoking in the most diverse regions and milieus. The manifestations of this renewal are varied: a profound communion of souls, intimate contact with God, in fidelity to the commitments undertaken at baptism, in prayer—frequently in group prayer—in which each person, expressing himself freely, aids, sustains and fosters the prayer of the others and, at the basis of everything, a personal conviction, which does not have its source solely in a teaching received by faith, but also in a certain lived experience. This lived experience shows that without God man can do nothing, that with him, on the other hand, everything becomes possible: hence this need to praise God, thank him, celebrate the marvels that he works everywhere about us and within us. Human existence rediscovers its "relationship to God," what is called the "vertical dimension," without which man is irremediably crippled. Not of course that this "search for God" appears as a desire for conquest or possession; it wishes to be a pure acceptance of him who loves us and gives himself freely to us, desiring, because he loves us, to communicate to us a life that we have to receive freely from him, but not without a humble fidelity on our part. And this fidelity must know how to unite action to faith according to the teaching of St. James: "For as the body apart from the spirit is dead, so faith apart from works is dead" (James 2, 26).

How then could this "spiritual renewal" not be a "chance" for the Church and for the world? And how, in this case, could one not take all the means to ensure that it remains so?

These means, dear sons and daughters, the Holy

Spirit will certainly wish to show you himself, according to the wisdom of those whom the Holy Spirit himself has established as "guardians, to feed the Church of God" (Acts 20, 28). For they are very precise directives, directives that we shall content ourself with recalling to you. To be faithful to them will be for you the best guarantee for the future.

You know the great importance that the apostle attributed to the "spiritual gifts." "Never try to suppress the Spirit," he wrote to the Thessalonians while immediately adding: "Test everything, hold fast what is good" (1 Thessalonians 5, 19. 21). Thus he considered that a discernment was always necessary, and he entrusted the task of testing to those whom he had placed over the community (cf. v. 12). With the Corinthians, a few years later, he enters into great detail: in particular, he indicates to them three principles in the light of which they will more easily be able to practice this indispensable discernment.

1. The first principle by which he begins his expose is fidelity to the authentic doctrine of the faith (1 Corinthians 12, 1-3). Anything that contradicted it would not come from the Spirit; he who distributes his gifts is the same one who inspired the Scriptures and who assists the living Magisterium of the Church, to whom, according to the Catholic faith, Christ entrusted the authentic interpretation of these Scriptures. This is why you experience the need for an ever deeper doctrinal formation: biblical, spiritual, theological. Only a formation such as this, whose authenticity must be guaranteed by the hierarchy, will preserve you from every possible deviation and give you the certitude and joy of having served the cause of the Gospel without "beating the air" (1 Corinthians 9, 26).

2. The second principle: all spiritual gifts are to be received with gratitude, and you know that the list is long (1 Corinthians 12, 4-10. 28-30), and does not claim to be complete (cf. Romans 12, 6-8; Ephesians 6, 11). Given, nevertheless, "for the common good" (1 Corinthians 12, 7), they do not all procure this common good to the same degree. Thus the Corinthians are to "desire the higher gifts" (1 Corinthians 12, 31), those most useful for the community (cf. 1 Corinthians 14, 1-5).

3. The third principle is the most important one in the thought of the apostle. This principle has suggested to him one of the most beautiful pages, without a doubt, in all literature, to which a recent translator has given an evocative title: "Above all hovers love" (E. Osty). No matter how desirable spiritual goods are— and they are desirable—only the love of charity, *agape*, makes the Christian perfect; it alone makes people pleasing to God—*gratia grantum faciens*, in the expression of the theologians. This love not only presupposes a gift of the Spirit; it implies the active presence of his person in the heart of the Christian. The Fathers of the Church commented on these verses, vying with one another to explain them. In the words of St. Fulgentius, to quote just one example: "The Holy Spirit can give every kind of gift without being present himself; on the other hand, he proves that he is present by grace when he gives love" (*se ipsum demonstrat per gratiam presentem, quando tribuit caritatem*) (*Contra Fabianum*, Fragment 28: *PL* 65, 791). Present in the soul, he communicates to it, with grace, the Most Blessed Trinity's own life, the very love with which the Father loves the Son in the Holy Spirit (John 17, 26), the love by which Christ has loved us and by which we, in our turn, can and must love our brethren, that is, "not only in word

or speech but in deed and in truth" (1 John 3, 18).

The tree is judged by its fruits, and St. Paul tells us that "the fruit of the Spirit is love" (Galatians 5, 22)— love such as he has just described in his hymn to love. It is to love that are ordered all the gifts which the Spirit distributes to whom he wills, for it is love which builds up (cf. 1 Corinthians 8, 1), just as it is love which, after Pentecost, made the first Christians into a community dedicated to fellowship (cf. Acts 2, 42), everyone being "of one heart and soul" (Acts 4, 32).

Be faithful to the directives of the great apostle. And, in accordance with the teaching of the same apostle, also be faithful to the frequent and worthy celebration of the Eucharist (cf. 1 Corinthians 11, 26-29). This is the way that the Lord has chosen in order that we may have his life in us (cf. John 6, 53). In the same way, approach with confidence the sacrament of reconciliation. These sacraments express that grace comes to us from God, through the necessary mediation of the Church.

Beloved sons and daughters, with the help of the Lord, strong in the intercession of Mary, Mother of the Church and in a communion of faith, charity and the apostolate with your pastors, you will be sure of not deceiving yourselves. And thus you will contribute, for your part, to the renewal of the Church.

Jesus is the Lord! Alleluia!

(*The Holy Father then said in English:*)

We are happy to greet you, dear sons and daughters, in the affection of Christ Jesus, and in his name to offer you a word of encouragement and exhortation for your Christian lives.

Lincoln Christian College

You have gathered here in Rome under the sign of the Holy Year; you are striving in union with the whole Church for renewal—spiritual renewal, authentic renewal, Catholic renewal, renewal in the Holy Spirit. We are pleased to see signs of this renewal: a taste for prayer, contemplation, praising God, attentiveness to the grace of the Holy Spirit, and more assiduous reading of the Sacred Scriptures. We know likewise that you wish to open your hearts to reconciliation with God and your fellow men.

For all of us this renewal and reconciliation is a further development of the grace of divine adoption, the grace of our sacramental baptism "into Christ Jesus" and "into his death" (Romans 6, 3), in order that we "might walk in newness of life" (Romans 6, 4).

Always give great importance to this sacrament of baptism and to the demands that it imposes. St. Paul is quite clear: "You must consider yourselves dead to sin but alive to God in Christ Jesus" (Romans 6, 11). This is the immense challenge of genuine sacramental Christian living, in which we must be nourished by the body and blood of Christ, renewed by the sacrament of penance, sustained by the grace of confirmation and refreshed by humble and persevering prayer. This is likewise the challenge of opening your hearts to your brethren in need. There are no limits to the challenge of love: the poor and needy and afflicted and suffering across the world and near at hand all cry out to you, as brothers and sisters of Christ, asking for the proof of your love, asking for the word of God, asking for bread, asking for life. They ask to see a reflection of Christ's own sacrificial, self-giving love—love for his Father and love for his brethren.

Lincoln Christian College

Yes, dear sons and daughters, this is the will of Jesus: that the world should see your good works, the goodness of your acts, the proof of your Christian lives, and glorify the Father who is in heaven (cf. Matthew 5, 16). This indeed is spiritual renewal and only through the Holy Spirit can it be accomplished. And this is why we do not cease to exhort you earnestly to "desire the higher gifts" (1 Corinthians 12, 31). This was our thought yesterday, when on the solemnity of Pentecost we said: "Yes, this is a day of joy, but also a day of resolve and determination: to open ourselves to the Holy Spirit, to remove what is opposed to his action, and to proclaim, in the Christian authenticity of our daily lives, that Jesus is Lord."

(Following is a translation of the Holy Father's address given in Italian:)

Very dear ones: It is permissible to add a few words in Italian (*applause*)—in fact, two messages. One is for those of you who are here with the charismatic pilgrimage. The other is for these pilgrims who are present by chance at this great assembly.

First, for you: reflect on the two words by which you are designated—"Spiritual Renewal." Where the Spirit is concerned we are immediately alert, immediately happy to welcome the coming of the Holy Spirit. More than that, we invite him, we pray to him, we desire nothing more than that Christians, believing people, should experience an awareness, a worship, a greater joy through the Spirit of God among us. Have we forgotten the Holy Spirit? Certainly not! We want him, we honor him, we love him, and we invoke him.

And you, with your devotion and fervor, you wish to live in the Spirit. (*applause*) And this should be where your second name comes in—a renewal. It ought to rejuvenate the world, give it back a spirituality, a soul, and religious thought; it ought to reopen its closed lips to prayer and open its mouth to song, to joy, to hymns, and to witnessing. It will be very fortuitous for our times, for our brothers, that there should be a generation, your generation of young people, who shout out to the world the glory and the greatness of the God of Pentecost. (*applause*) In the hymn which we read this morning in the breviary, and which dates back as far as St. Ambrose in the third or fourth century, there is this phrase which is hard to translate and should be very simple: *laeti*, that means "joyfully," *bibamus*, "we absorb," *sobriam*, that means "well-defined and well-moderated," *profusionem spiritus*, "the outpouring of the Spirit." *Laeti bibamus sobriam profusionem spiritus*. It could be a formula impressed over your movement: a plan and an approval of the movement.

The second message is for those pilgrims present at this great assembly who do not belong to your movement. They should unite themselves with you to celebrate the feast of Pentecost—the spiritual renewal of the world, of our society, and of our souls—so that they too, devout pilgrims to this center of the Catholic faith, might nourish themselves on the enthusiasm and the spiritual energy with which we must live our religion. And we will say only this: today, either one lives one's faith with devotion, depth, energy, and joy or that faith will die out.

Statement on Catholic Charismatic Renewal by
the Committee for Pastoral Research and Practices
National Conference of Catholic Bishops, U.S.A.
Washington, D.C., United States Catholic
    Conference 1975

Introduction

In an effort to discharge their pastoral responsibility to guide the flock of Christ entrusted to their care, the bishops of the United States asked the Committee on Pastoral Research and Practices to prepare a statement on the charismatic renewal.

The present document is a response to that request. It is pastoral in tone and content. It is not an exhaustive treatment. It simply points up certain directions and enunciates certain principles. A more complete treatment of the matter may be desirable at some future time which would deal in greater depth with the charismatic renewal as it is developing in the United States. The full text of an address of Pope Paul VI on the subject added here in the form of an appendix gives valuable and additional insights into this timely topic.

This statement, then, is offered by the Committee on Pastoral Research and Practices in the hope that it may be of service to bishops, priests, and lay people in their effort to "test everything and retain what is good" (1 Thessalonians 5, 21) and to fulfill the apostolic injunction to "set your hearts on the greater gifts," above all on "the way which surpasses all others" (1 Corinthians 12, 31; 13, 1).

Statement on Charismatic Renewal

1. The Second Vatican Council's *Constitution on the Church* teaches that the Holy Spirit sanctifies and leads the Church not only through the sacraments and ministries, "but, allotting his gifts to everyone according as he wills, he distributes special graces among the faithful of every rank. By these gifts he makes them fit and ready to undertake the various tasks and duties which contribute toward the renewal and building up of the Church, according to the words of the apostle, 'The manifestation of the Spirit is given to everyone for profit' (1 Corinthians 12, 7). These charisms, whether they be the more outstanding or the more simple and widely diffused, are to be received with thanksgiving and consolation, for they are especially suited to and useful for the needs of the Church. Extraordinary gifts are not to be rashly sought after nor are the fruits of apostolic labor to be presumptuously expected from their use. Judgment as to their genuineness and proper use belongs to those who hold authority in the Church and to whose special competence it belongs, not indeed to extinguish the Spirit, but to test all things and hold fast to that which is good" (*Lumen Gentium*, n. 12).

2. It is clear, then, that these gifts or charisms have been given to the Church from the beginning and cannot be said to belong only to our times. The Church is a living, growing reality precisely because of the continual and vital action of the Holy Spirit sent by the Father and the Son.

3. Because it is not self-evident which manifestations are truly from the Holy Spirit, it is necessary that the members of the Church in communion with their pastors be conscious of the possibility of self-deception and of the need to keep in mind the wise norms handed

down in the written word of God and the perennial teaching of the Church. First of all, there is the saying of our Lord himself, "You will know them by their deeds" (Matthew 7, 16). This does not mean that such gifts as tongues, miracles or prophecies are the "deeds" or "fruits" by which the Spirit can be recognized. It is these very things which must be judged and discerned. Hence when our Lord speaks of the test of "deeds" as providing the sign of truth and authenticity he is speaking of conformity with the full teaching of the Gospel and the following of his example. The apostle Paul in the New Testament enlarges on this teaching of the Lord when he affirms that the fruit of the Spirit is "love, joy, peace, patient endurance, kindness, faith, mildness and chastity" (Galatians 5, 22). He also explains that the authentic gifts of the Spirit are always for the building up of the Church in unity and charity, "Make every effort to preserve the unity which has the Spirit as its origin and peace as its binding force" (Ephesians 4, 3). He then adds, "Each of us has received God's favor in the measure in which Christ bestows it. . . . It is he who gave apostles, prophets, evangelists, pastors and teachers in roles of service for the faithful to build up the body of Christ" (Ephesians 4, 7. 11-12).

He states the same thing with equal emphasis in writing to the Corinthians, "To each person the manifestation of the Spirit is given for the common good" (1 Corinthians 12, 7).

The greatest authenticating sign of the Spirit, however, is love—not any kind of love but that kind of sacrificial, Christian love described in these words: "Love is patient; love is kind. Love is not jealous, it does not put on airs, it is not snobbish. Love is never rude, it is not self-seeking, it is not prone to anger; neither does it brood over injuries. Love does not rejoice in what is wrong but rejoices with the truth. There is no limit to love's forebearance, to its trust, its hope, its power to endure. Love never fails. Prophecies will cease, tongues will be silent, knowledge will pass away. . . . There are in the end three things that last: faith, hope and love, and the greatest of these is love" (1 Corinthians 13, 4-8. 13).

Lastly, we must mention one more authenticating sign of the Spirit found both in the Gospel and in the apostolic letters of the New Testament—namely that the Spirit always bears witness to Jesus. "The Holy Spirit whom the Father will send in my name will instruct you in everything and remind you of all that I told you" (John 14, 26). "When he comes, however, being the Spirit of truth, he will guide you to all truth. He will not speak on his own, but will speak only what he hears. . . . In doing this he will give glory to me, because he will have received from me what he will announce to you" (John 16, 13-14).

4. These norms given in the word of God must be brought to bear in making judgment about the action of the Holy Spirit. In addition it is clear that the authentic action of the Holy Spirit can never be in conflict with the authentic teaching of the Church since it is one and the same Spirit who pours out the gifts in all the faithful and who guides and sustains the teaching authority of the Church. St. Augustine, in this connection, affirms: "We have the Holy Spirit to the extent that we love the Church" (Tract. in John XXXII, 8: CCL XXXVI, 304). It is also important to turn to the great saints and masters of the spiritual life whose own experience under the guidance of the Holy Spirit has bequeathed to the Church of every age a rich treasury of discernment and wisdom. Outstanding in these

things are saints like Gregory the Great, Ignatius Loyola, Teresa of Avila and John of the Cross.

5. One of the great manifestations of the Spirit in our times has been the Second Vatican Council. Many believe also that the Catholic charismatic renewal is another such manifestation of the Spirit. It does indeed offer many positive signs, clearer in some groups than in others. Where the movement is making solid progress there is a strongly grounded spirit of faith in Jesus Christ as Lord. This in turn leads to a renewed interest in prayer, both private and group prayer. Many of those who belong to the movement experience a new sense of spiritual values, a heightened consciousness of the action of the Holy Spirit, the praise of God and a deepening personal commitment to Christ. Many, too, have grown in devotion to the Eucharist and partake more fruitfully in the sacramental life of the Church. Reverence for the Mother of the Lord takes on fresh meaning and many feel a deeper sense of and attachment to the Church. Things of this kind certainly merit encouragement and reflect the biblical and Church teaching mentioned above.

6. It is understandable that any new movement will face difficulties and involve a certain mixture of desirable and undesirable elements. A previous report from this committee pointed out some dangers which continue to exist here and there, and which cannot be ignored if the movement is to develop in a positive and fruitful way. Elitism and that kind of biblical fundamentalism which offend against the authenticating norms of Sacred Scripture and the teaching of the Church are two of these dangers. Elitism creates a closed circle and gives rise to divisions rather than unity and charity, and biblical fundamentalism does not do justice to the mission of the Holy Spirit to bear witness

to "all Jesus has taught." There is also the danger for some who are involved in this movement to ignore the intellectual and doctrinal content of faith and reduce it to a felt religious experience.

It is in the hope that the truly positive values of the charismatic renewal will prevail, and that the movement may in fact contribute as all authentic action of the Holy Spirit does "to building up the Church" in unity and charity, that we feel it important to direct attention to these dangers and undesirable features which continue to appear in some groups.

Other aspects of the charismatic renewal which call for caution are such things as healing, prophecy, praying in tongues, and the interpretation of tongues. It cannot be denied that such phenomena could be genuine manifestations of the Spirit. These things, however, must be carefully scrutinized, and their importance, even if genuine, should not be exaggerated.

7. The charismatic renewal cannot live or be productive in isolation. It has to have a strong bond with the total life of the Church. This means that it is necessary to maintain involvement in the local parish community as a whole and to seek out and work under the guidance of the parish priests who as sharers in the pastoral ministry of the bishop have responsibility for coordinating the overall well-being of the parish. Priests and bishops, of course, have the correlative responsibility to develop means for relating the charismatic renewal to the whole Church.

8. In order to develop a climate of mutual understanding, trust and communication, personal contact by bishops and priests with both leaders and members of the various groups is essential. Once this relationship is established it can be effectively sustained by the ap-

pointment of diocesan liaison persons who can keep current with developments in the movement, offer sound guidance, and keep the ordinaries informed.

9. The parishes should be encouraged to integrate the existing charismatic groups into their structures so that effective communication is maintained. It would be helpful if the priests of the parish would have continuing communication with the leaders in their parish. Leaders should be open to the insights and suggestions of the parish priests, and they, in turn, should try to encourage what is good and positive in the groups they come in contact with, as well as to point out what they believe to be undesirable or harmful either to individuals or to the movement or to the parish itself. Effective guidance, then, will require the encouragement of positive goals and ideals while working out problem areas in frank consultation with leaders and members of the group.

10. Association with priestly leadership is clearly essential to the healthy development of the charismatic renewal. And so we strongly encourage priests to take an interest in the movement. Because of his unique role and the charism of sacred ordination, the priest can most effectively relate the work of the renewal to the total life of the Church and in this way fulfill his own special function of coordinator of the gifts of the Spirit.

Priests who have not personally shared in the movement itself should, of course, be cautious in making judgments or decisions and should make sure that they are fully informed and understand what is taking place. At the same time there is a healthy factor in openness on the part of the members of the movement to those who are not part of it, since this offers an element of objectivity which is always valuable.

11. A key element in the future success of the charismatic movement is the formation of leaders who are well grounded in the teaching of the Church and in the understanding of Scripture, leaders who are open to one another and mature enough to share responsibility. In many places the benefits derived from such leadership are already markedly visible. Regular participation of local leaders in regional and national meetings of the Catholic charismatic renewal should prove helpful also.

12. An especially sensitive pastoral question concerns charismatic groups which involve both Catholics and Christians of other traditions. Such groups merit special pastoral interest. Continual or exclusive participation in ecumenical groups runs the risk of diluting the sense of Catholic identity. On the other hand, occasional ecumenical sharing in prayer groups can be beneficial. Catholics who participate in such groups should be mature in their faith and committed to the principles of Catholic belief. They should be well informed of and careful to follow the Church's guidelines for ecumenical activity.

13. Because the charismatic renewal is new to most Catholics, bishops and other pastors can offer much needed assistance when difficulties arise between the movement and other Church groups and institutions. The legitimate concerns of all should be examined and reconciled through dialogue based on the spirit and teaching of the Gospel and the example of Christ. Pastors may also at times be helpful in assisting leaders of the movement to resolve conflicts within charismatic groups themselves. The peaceful development of the movement which we wish to encourage will be fostered if less mature persons are only permitted to

involve themselves under the special direction of the more mature. This reflects the teaching and experience of St. Paul who counseled, "The spirits of the prophets are under the prophets' control, since God is a God, not of confusion, but of peace" (1 Corinthians 14, 32-33).

14. A more recent development in the renewal is the establishment of small communities in which members of the movement live together in order to deepen their life in the Spirit. The success of these communities depends on mature leadership, on careful fidelity to the norms mentioned in the earlier part of this paper and on a strong link with ecclesial community. Regular and objective evaluation with outside help is very important. In his closing address to the World Synod of Bishops on October 26, 1974, the Holy Father encouraged the development of small communities but called for a sense of balance: "In addition we have noted with satisfaction the hope furnished by small communities and the reminder they give of the work of the Holy Spirit. But this hope would be truly stunted if their ecclesial life, in the organic unity of the single body of Christ, were to cease or be exempted from legitimate ecclesiastical authority or be left to the arbitrary impulse of individuals."

15. To the members of the movement, then, to pastors and to all the faithful of Christ, we commend the words of Scripture which we take as our own guiding light: "Do not stifle the Spirit. Do not despise prophecies. Test everything; retain what is good. Avoid any semblance of evil" (1 Thessalonians 5, 19-22). We encourage those who already belong, and we support the positive and desirable directions of the charismatic renewal.

On Primary Needs of the Church
Address of Pope Paul VI, October 16, 1974

If we persist in posing again the question, which we have already raised several times, about the primary needs of the Church, we arrive at something extremely evident, which seems almost a tautology, as if we should say that a living being needs above all to live. Well, we dare to refer this paradoxical question to the Church to discover the essential principle that confers its primary raison d'être, its deep and indispensable animation. And here we reach an answer that gives us the key to this reality. The key is a mystery: the Church lives by the outpouring of the Holy Spirit, which we call grace, that is to say, a gift par excellence, charity, the Father's love, communicated to us by virtue of the redemption operated by Christ, in the Holy Spirit. Let us recall St. Augustine's synthesis: "What the soul is for the human body, the Holy Spirit is for the body of Christ, which is the Church" (Serm. 267; P.L. 38, 1231).

This is a well-known truth that we have all heard repeated and proclaimed by the recent Council: "When the work which the Father had given the Son to do on earth (cf. John 17, 4) was accomplished, the Holy Spirit was sent on the day of Pentecost in order that he might forever sanctify the Church, and thus all believers would have access to the Father through Christ in the one Spirit (cf. Ephesians 2, 18). He is the Spirit of life. . . . The Spirit dwells in the Church and in the hearts of the faithful as in a temple (cf. 1 Corinthians 3, 16; 6, 19). In them he prays and bears witness to the fact that they are adopted sons (cf. Galatians 4, 6; Romans 8, 15-16. 26). The Spirit guides the Church into the fullness of truth (cf. John 16, 13) and gives it a unity of fellowship and service. He furnishes and directs it with various gifts, both hierarchical and charismatic, and adorns it with the fruits of his grace (cf. Ephesians 4, 11-12; 1 Corinthians 12, 4; Galatians 4, 22). By the power of the Gospel he makes the Church grow and perpetually renews her" (*Lumen Gentium*, n. 4).

Learning from the Saints

This is a magnificent doctrine, which seems like a ladder coming down from the infinite and inaccessible mystery of divine life in itself, the Trinity, placing at the center of the divine plans and human destinies Christ's work of redemption, and drawing from it an extraordinary revelation, accessible to us in some way, the communion of our human lives with an order of salvation and goodness, which is the order of grace. From this order there appears a plan of unity and supernatural charity, and there spreads a resplendent economy of holiness, in which human events, psychology especially and moral and spiritual phenomenology, become a marvelous garden of superhuman beauty and variety.

These are well-known truths or truths that should be better known, because from the ordinary information we have about them the most important thing is lacking, the analysis of holiness, as it gushes forth from the vital breath of grace. Here we would have a first recommendation to make in this connection: knowledge of the lives of the saints. If in the past they offered a delightful pasture for popular culture and for the edifying fancy of devout people, for us today, trained in historical studies and psychological criticisms, they could offer a museum of incomparable human experiences and exciting examples for the possible progress of a real

moral and spiritual improvement. Remember: "Si isti
et istae, cur non ego?" (If these men and women could
do it, why can't I?)

Necessity of Grace

But we must immediately remember that grace is
necessary (a divine intervention, transcending the natural order), both for our personal salvation and for the
fulfillment of the plan of redemption for the whole
Church and all mankind, whom God's mercy calls to
salvation (cf. 1 Timothy 2, 4). Let us refer to the great
chapter on the doctrine on grace and justification, of
which the Council of Trent had so much to say (cf.
Denz.-Sch. 1520-1583), and which modern theology
still discusses as a subject of supreme interest. The necessity of grace presupposes an absolute need on the
part of man—the need that the miracle of Pentecost
should continue in the history of the Church and of the
world. It must continue in the double form with which
the gift of the Holy Spirit is granted to men, to sanctify
them in the first place (and this is the primary and indispensable form by which man becomes the object of
God's love—"gratum faciens," as the theologians say),
and to enrich them with special prerogatives, which we
call charisms ("gratis data"), in relation to the good of
their neighbor and especially of the community of the
faithful (cf. S. Th., I-II, III:4). A great deal is said
about charisms today, and, taking into account the
complexity and delicacy of such a subject, we cannot
but hope that a new abundance, not only of grace, but
also of charisms, will still be granted to the Church of
God today (cf. the recent study by Cardinal L. J. Suenens: "Une Nouvelle Pentecote?").

Work of the Spirit

At present we will just recall the main conditions on the part of man to receive God's gift par excellence, which is the Holy Spirit, who, as we know, "blows where it wills" (John 3, 8), but does not refuse the longing of those who wait for him, call him and welcome him (even though this longing itself comes from a deep inspiration of his). What are these conditions? Let us simplify the difficult answer by saying that the capacity to receive this "dulcis hospes animae" calls for faith, for humility and repentance, and normally for a sacramental act. Moreover, in the practice of our religious life it demands silence, meditation, listening, and above all invocation and prayer, as the apostles did with Mary in the upper room. It is necessary to be able to wait, to be able to call: Come, O Creator Spirit; come, O Holy Spirit!

If the Church is able to enter a phase of similar preparation for the new and perennial coming of the Holy Spirit, he, the "light of hearts," will not hesitate to give himself for the joy, the light, the fortitude, the apostolic virtue and unitive charity, which the Church needs today.

And so may it be, with our apostolic blessing.

Bibliography

Ahern, Barnabas. *New Horizons,* Notre Dame, Fides, 1963

Byrne, James. *Threshold of God's Promise: An Introduction to the Catholic Pentecostal Movement*, Notre Dame, Ave Maria, 1970

Christenson, Larry. *A Charismatic Approach to Social Action*, Minneapolis, Bethany Fellowship, 1974

Durrwell, F. X. *The Resurrection*, New York, Sheed and Ward, 1960

Ford, J. Massyngberde. *Ministries and Fruits of the Holy Spirit*, Notre Dame, Catholic Action Office, 1973

Gelpi, Donald. *Pentecostalism: A Theological Viewpoint*, New York, Paulist, 1971

Gheon, Henri. *The Secret of the Curé d'Ars*, New York, Sheed and Ward, 1938

Malatesta, Edward, *et al. Discernment of Spirits,* Collegeville, Liturgical Press, 1970

Martin, Ralph. *Unless the Lord Build the House. . . . The Church and the New Pentecost*, Notre Dame, Ave Maria, 1971

McDonnell, Kilian. "Catholic Pentecostalism: Problems in Evaluation," *Dialog* 9 (1970), pp. 35-54; reprinted as pamphlet by Dove Publications, Pecos, N.M.

————*Baptism in the Spirit as an Ecumenical Problem*, Notre Dame, 1972

McKenna, John H. *Eucharist and Holy Spirit: The Eucharistic Epiclesis in 20th Century Theology*, published for the Alcuin Club. Great Wakering, Mayhew-McCrimmon, 1975

O'Connor, Edward. *The Pentecostal Movement in the Catholic Church*, Notre Dame, Ave Maria Press, 1970

————(ed.) Summa Theologica, Vol. 24, *The Gifts of the Holy Spirit*, New York, McGraw-Hill, 1975

Rahner, Karl. *The Dynamic Element in the Church*, New York, Herder, 1964

Schillebeeckx, E. *Christ the Sacrament of the Encounter with God*, New York, Sheed and Ward, 1963

Spicq, Ceslaus. *Agape in the New Testament* (three volumes), translated by McNamara and Richter, St. Louis, B. Herder, 1963.

Suenens, Leon Joseph Cardinal. *A New Pentecost?* Translation by Scabury Press. London, Darton, Longman & Todd, 1975

Sullivan, Francis A. *The Pentecostal Movement*, Rome, Gregorian University Press, 1972

———*"Baptism in the Holy Spirit": A Catholic Interpretation of the Pentecostal Experience*, Rome, Gregorian University Press, 1974

Tugwell, Simon. *Did You Receive the Spirit?* New York, Paulist, 1972

Notes

1. "All were filled with the Holy Spirit. They began to express themselves in foreign tongues and make bold proclamation as the Spirit prompted them." (Acts 2, 4) "As I began to address them the Holy Spirit came upon them, just as it had upon us at the beginning." (Acts 11, 15) "As Paul laid his hands on them, the Holy Spirit came down on them and they began to speak in tongues and to utter prophecies." (Acts 19, 6)

2. For a contemporary commentary on St. Thomas' treatment of the gifts, see Edward D. O'Connor (ed.), *Summa Theologica*, Vol. 24, *The Gifts of the Holy Spirit* (New York, McGraw-Hill, 1975).

3. "Yes, God so loved the world that he gave his only Son, that whoever believes in him may not die but may have eternal life." (John 3, 16)

4. See F. X. Durrwell, *The Resurrection*, (New York: Sheed and Ward, 1960), pp. 98-103.

5. *Ibid.*, pp. 103-105. Cf. also, Karl Rahner, *The Dynamic Element in the Church* (New York: Herder, 1964), pp. 48ff.

6. Barnabas M. Ahern, *New Horizons* (Notre Dame: Fides, 1963), pp. 75-79.

7. For a most thorough treatise on agape, see Ceslaus Spicq, *Agape in the New Testament*, 3 vols. (St. Louis: B. Herder, 1963).

8. "It was in one Spirit that all of us, whether Jew or Greek, slave or free, were baptized into one body. All of us have been given to drink of the one Spirit." (1 Cor. 12, 13) "Make every effort to preserve the unity which has the Spirit as its origin." (Ephesians 4, 3)

9. "He who hardens his heart will fall into evil." (Prov-

erbs 28, 14) "Despite his many signs performed in their presence, they refused to believe in him. This was to fulfill the word of the prophet Isaiah . . . He has blinded their eyes, and numbed their hearts." (John 12, 37-40)

10. "As a consequence, your faith rests not on the wisdom of men but on the power of God." (1 Corinthians 2, 5) Cf. 1 Corinthians 1, 18-25.

11. "Go into the whole world and proclaim the good news to all creation. The man who believes in it and accepts baptism will be saved; the man who refuses to believe in it will be condemned." (Mark 16, 15-16) Cf. Matthew 28, 18.

12. Today an increasing number of liturgists and theologians urge that the now separated sacraments of initiation (baptism, confirmation and the Eucharist) be reintegrated into a single rite to be administered in infancy, childhood or adulthood, properly celebrated in the midst of a congregation. For a scholarly treatise of this topic, see *Made, Not Born: New Perspectives on Christian Initiation and the Catechumenate* (Notre Dame: University of Notre Dame Press, 1976).

13. See Galatians 5, 16-26.

14. Durrwell, *op. cit.*, pp. 103-105.

15. For an outstanding contemporary treatise of this subject, see John H. McKenna, *Eucharist and Holy Spirit* (Great Wakering: Mayhew-McCrimmon, 1975).

16. See Donald L. Gelpi, *Pentecostalism, A Theological Viewpoint* (New York: Paulist Press, 1971), pp. 8-42.

17. Francis A. Sullivan, *Baptism in the Holy Spirit* (Rome: Gregorian University Press, 1974), p. 60.

18. Simon Tugwell, *Did You Receive the Spirit?* (New York: Paulist Press, 1972), p. 67.

19. *Ibid.*, p. 62

20. Gelpi, *op. cit.*, pp. 135-136.

21. For an evaluation of the involvement of charismatics in social action programs, see Joseph M. Fichter. *Catholic Cult of the Paraclete* (New York: Sheed and Ward, 1974), pp. 80-98.

22. See Leon Joseph Cardinal Suenens, *A New Pentecost?* (London: Darton, Longman & Todd, 1975), p. 111.

23. Francis A. Sullivan, *The Pentecostal Movement*

(Rome: Gregorian University Press, 1972), p. 241.

24. Henri Gheon, *The Secret of the Curé d'Ars* (New York: Sheed and Ward, 1938), p. 53.

25. For a commentary on St. Ignatius' views, see Edward Malatesta *et al.*, *Discernment of Spirits* (Collegeville: Liturgical Press, 1970), pp. 80-91.

26. See also Matthew 16, 21-25.

27. For an excellent summary of these principles, see Malatesta, *op. cit.*, pp. 105-112.

28. For a thorough development of this theme, see Suenens, *op. cit.*

Subject Index

231.1
Or7